The Growth of World Law

THE GROWTH OF WORLD LAW

By *Percy E. Corbett*

PRINCETON, NEW JERSEY

PRINCETON UNIVERSITY PRESS

1971

LC Card: 70-132236

ISBN: 0-691-09223-0

This book has been composed in Linotype Caledonia

Printed in the United States of America

by Princeton University Press

To my colleagues and students at Lehigh University

CONTENTS

ACKNOWLEDGMENTS

THE friends who have read all or parts of this book and offered useful suggestions are too numerous to list here. In any case, some of them might prefer to remain anonymous. But special thanks are due to Professor Charles Hendel of Yale, with whom over the years I have discussed the whole subject matter. The Department of International Relations at Lehigh not only provided running commentary, but permitted me to include in Chapter 7, "From International to World Law," a revised version of my paper under the same title in its series of Research Monographs. For expert secretarial assistance, I am indebted to Mrs. Doris Wilkinson and Miss Priscilla Bryan. Finally, nothing could be more kindly or more dedicated than the help always given me by the Pliny Fisk staff in Princeton's Firestone Library.

Lehigh University   PERCY E. CORBETT
May 1970

ABBREVIATIONS

ADI Rec.	Academie de Droit International, *Recueil des Cours*
AJIL	*American Journal of International Law*
ASIL	American Society of International Law
CECA	European Coal and Steel Community
CEE	European Economic Community
DSB	*Department of State Bulletin*
Euratom	European Atomic Energy Community
GAOR	*General Assembly Official Records*
IBRD	International Bank for Reconstruction and Development
ICC	International Chamber of Commerce
ICJ	International Court of Justice
ILC	International Law Commission of the United Nations
ILO	International Labor Organization
LNTS	League of Nations Treaty Series
LQR	*Law Quarterly Review*
Multilateral Treaties	Multilateral Treaties in respect of which the Secretary-General performs Depositary Functions
OAS	Organization of American States
OAU	Organization of African Unity
ONUC	United Nations Operation in the Congo
PCIJ	Permanent Court of International Justice
SACDT	Southeast Asia Collective Defense Treaty

The Growth of World Law

INTRODUCTION

THIS book is a study of the development of legal institutions transcending the state and constituting the still weak framework of a community embracing humanity as a whole. Beginning with a brief discussion of the general principles and structures by which men have sought to achieve order and justice, it surveys the long effort to construct a system to govern the conduct of states as distinct entities. Then, after exploring areas of international activity where practice is still anarchic, it goes on to examine, in succession, the move in the last half century to strengthen the international normative order with agencies of administration, adjudication, and enforcement; the gradual assimilation of national legal systems; and the recent effort to endow every human being with rights enforceable against his own and foreign governments.

What is presented here is not a design for utopia. It is an account of things that have happened and are happening, coupled with a search for trends. There is of course no escaping the fact that one's predispositions go a long way toward determining what he sees in history, and if any disciple of Niebuhr, let us say, happens to read what I have written, he may well find my optimism gratuitously idealistic. Actually, I find myself in agreement with Niebuhr's constant warning that a working community of mankind cannot be created by fiat. Where I do not follow him is in his belittlement of the liberal's faith in progress, and

3

in his extreme skepticism about man's ultimate ability to establish institutions capable of rendering him service on the universal plane commensurate with that now rendered by the state in the national community. Not being obsessed with original sin, and full of wonder at the civilization that the human animal has been able to contrive, I find in history no more basis for the conclusion that he cannot learn to control international violence and to live under supranational law than for the belief that he can do so in a decade or a generation.

Legal writers have not been wanting among the prophets and advocates of a world community freed from the scourge of war and serving the collective welfare, if not from a sense of brotherhood, then from a conviction of common interest. Some of them, with scant attention to the profound changes in human attitudes and perceptions that alone can make such a community possible, have projected commonwealths hardly less millennial than the collective hyper-person that Teilhard de Chardin saw as the final product of evolution. Happily, law has not been quite proof against utopian idealism. In the development of law, however, the characteristic role of the jurist has been the careful adjustment of existing institutions to new needs. He does not set out to reshape immediately "this sorry scheme of things entire." If his aim is progress, he would have it without revolutionary disruption.

This disciplined and gradual technique will not deliver us from our immediate peril. To avert the present danger of extinction, our civilization has nothing more reliable to count upon than the voluntary restraint of the nuclear-armed states. But if we would use any time so granted us to carry on with the construction of a system which, if we survive the present threat, may prevent its recurrence and provide lasting security, we cannot dispense with the formulative work of the lawyer.

Eight years before the Second World War, H. G. Wells, qualifying an earlier prognosis that "the salvaging of civilization was a race between education and catastrophe" saw catastrophe rushing upon his world while the saving education had not even started.[1] Four decades later, the dimension of threatening catastrophe would have taxed even his prophetic imagination. And, though the necessary education has at least left the starting post, it still has far to go to exorcise war from the minds of men. With education must come crucial political decisions. Even in these fundamental processes, the lawyer, as I shall try to show, has a necessary part. His peculiar technical usefulness lies, however, in the formulation, interpretation, and application of rules, and in designing and remodelling the structures of power and authority to meet social needs as they arise. What he has done in the past, is doing now, and will continue doing in this domain, is the central theme of my study.

[1] *After Democracy* (London, 1932), p. 217.

1.

LAW, COMMUNITY, AND ORDER

THOUGH clearly essential to the organization, operation, and progressive development of community, law cannot create it.[1] The indispensable beginning is a sense, however unreasoned and inarticulate, of common interest. Law registers and consolidates the degree of community achieved in commands, prohibitions, and organization that express the general feeling as to how members of the community should behave, and what should be done in case of violation. Primitive societies abound in such imperatives, some the product of custom, some ascribed to divine command, some enacted by conscious decision.[2] Wherever their violation may be followed by penalties approved by the community, there is, in my terminology, at the least an inchoate legal order.

Order, in the sense of regulated behavior, is observable in all groups of living things. Below the human level it is a product of instinct; in man it is the response to a common sense of need. Anthropology has revealed its mounting complexity in prehistoric man. The need, or interest, may be success in the hunt; it may be defense or aggression against other groups; it may be, as in the earliest Mesopotamian civilization, organized group labor to increase the

[1] For a classic statement of the role of law in the human community, see R. M. MacIver, *The Modern State* (Oxford, 1932), p. 149.
[2] Cf. Robert H. Lowie, *The Origin of the State* (New York, 1962); E. A. Hoebel, *The Law of Primitive Man* (Cambridge, Mass., 1954).

food supply through irrigation.[3] Whatever the immediate purpose, the incipient order leads to a division of labor, to the evolution of a ruling class, priestly or military, to guilds of skilled artisans released by the food surplus from the labor of hunting or cultivation, to the arts and sciences, and to the building of cities.

As cities grew in size and number and their civilization became ever more complex and demanding, order beyond their boundaries—a measure of regulation governing exchanges between communities—was an imperative need. The first mode of meeting this need was probably conquest; but always the expanding community met others in its path, and an alternative to perpetual war had to be found in agreements defining at least temporarily the limits of rule and the terms of truce. The earliest sculpture and writing record embassies, treaties, and alliances. Here already was a realization of interest common to distinct communities, the first step toward a community of communities. The drive for order in an expanding group, from family through clan to polis and beyond, has been a leitmotif of human history.

Leagues uniting cities were an early characteristic of Hellenic civilization. At first of a religious character, providing for the joint maintenance and celebration of a common cult, these later took on political features for the limitation of violence, settlement of disputes, and common defense. Yet the Hellenes failed to establish a lasting collective order. Soon after the Delian League had saved Athens and her allies from the onslaughts of Persia, the attempt to turn the League into an Athenian empire led to the Peloponnesian War and the disintegration of the fragile unity which was all that the proud sovereignty of the city-states would endure. As in our day, the sense of community was

[3] Cf. W. H. McNeill, *The Rise of the West: A History of the Human Community* (New York, 1963), pp. 29-40.

too weak to overcome the short-sighted particularism that has been the time-honored accompaniment of political organization. The influence of Greece upon subsequent thought and action moving towards universal institutions was less one of practical demonstration than of theory. Her philosophers had conceived and immortalized ideas of human brotherhood and natural law which the Hellenes were never to implement, but which were to be a source of inspiration invoked from their time to ours.

Throughout the Middle Ages the Church was the strongest influence making for European order. In his *Civitas Dei*, St. Augustine had cast the Church in this role, and from his distinction between just and unjust war sprang a discussion of the rights and duties of princes that was eventually to form the early literature of international law. Ecclesiastical writers, with the scholar's yearning for peace, preserved the lore of *jus naturae* and *jus gentium* as laws governing all men, including sovereigns. The truce of God and the sanctuary of His temples offered occasional mitigation of armed barbarity. But neither the casuistry of the just and unjust war, nor the sanctionless precepts of natural law, could impose reliable restraint upon potentates avid for the spoils of victory; and the Holy Roman Empire, temporal counterpart of the Church, had little control over even its weaker vassals. Long before the Reformation divided European Christianity into warring sects, endemic violence had demonstrated the fatal weakness of the most solemn precepts unsupported by force.

In the lay, bourgeois world of commerce, where violence was an enemy rather than a mode of profit, a measure of regularity and predictability was derived from the law merchant, a tradition of order, with its roots in the ancient Rhodian sea law, partially and variably codified in such collections as the *Consolato del Mare*, the *Laws of Oleron*, and the *Leges Wisbuenses*.

9

All these doctrines, customs, and institutions, ecclesiastical and lay, amounted to little more than the elementary fragments of a legal system. They were enough, however, to inspire visions of a universal order in which power would be the servant of law. This is the image that philosophers, poets, and priests, from the Greek Stoics to the world federalists of our time, have held up to humanity as the ultimate goal of political organization. Always the vision stood in sharp contrast with the turbulent reality of international relations, and the contrast has hardly softened in the half century since plans of universal organization to keep the peace and share the skilled exploitation of resources ceased to be a monopoly of the dreamers and became part of the declared policy of governments.

"World order" is now a term of everyday use in the discussion of international affairs. As used in this book, it has a connotation different from that of "*the* world order," "*the* international order," "*the* international system." These three terms are used more or less interchangeably to signify the existing pattern of relationships between states, whereas "world order," without the definite article, has in it the suggestion of possibility and aspiration, as of something toward which present phenomena are being directed or are of their own momentum converging. The image projected is one of human behavior regulated by law on a world scale in much the same way as it is now regulated within the state. The order contemplated is supranational, but its subjects and actors are not necessarily states alone; they may be other groupings or even individuals. World order presumes world community under law; but this is not necessarily a community of states; it may be a community of individuals, transcending states.

Contemporary philosophers and scientists have painted alluring pictures of man and his institutions in a coming world community which, they seem confident, is not to be nipped in the bud by nuclear annihilation. The citizens of this universal commonwealth are to be a transformed breed of humans, freed from that passionate devotion to selfish interests that characterizes their present ancestor, and living in peaceful and productive cooperation. For the late Teilhard de Chardin, indeed, the whole process of evolution was to culminate in an ultrahuman composite person embracing mankind—a prospect that even so secular a thinker as Sir Julian Huxley commends to our serious contemplation.[4]

Such visions of remote millennia tell us little about the possibility and the means of averting immediate perils that make it less than certain that the race has any future, good or bad. They will nevertheless serve man well if they help to sustain faith in his potentialities and the measure of idealism it breeds. Without these supplements to motives of mere expediency there would be little incentive to continue even the fumbling half measures by which we try to control the forces threatening to destroy us.

With these half measures some of the philosophers have little patience. Karl Jaspers, for instance, was outspoken in his contempt for the United Nations as a transparent veil for the hypocrisies of governments still exclusively dedicated to national ends. Following a merciless analysis of *Realpolitik*, this assessment of what many of us continue to regard, despite all its weaknesses, as the chief hope of progress towards an operative world community, leaves us somewhat unprepared for Jaspers' apparent belief in a coming regenerate human self participating in a universal communion of reason.[5] Apart from the restraints that they

[4] Pierre Teilhard de Chardin, *Le Phénomène Humain* (Paris, 1955), trans. Bernard Wall as *The Phenomenon of Man* (New York, 1959), introd. Julian Huxley; and *L'Avenir de L'Homme* (Paris, 1959), pp. 353-395.

[5] *The Future of Mankind*, E. B. Ashton's translation of Karl Jaspers'

11

sometimes contrive to impose upon violence and the inadequate but measurable contributions that they make to
man's welfare, are not our proliferating international agencies schools for reason?

Arnold Toynbee is something of a bridge between the
transcendentalists and those who grapple, against appalling odds, with the international problems confronting us
here and now. He has nothing like Jaspers' lofty contempt
for our developing international institutions, which he
would strengthen to the point of taking away the power of
states to make war and reducing those traditional centers
of sovereignty to the role of local government. He suggests
that all the figuratively universal states found in his vast
survey of history have been trial runs for a literally universal state that is "no longer below our horizon." There is, to
be sure, a millennial tone to his warning that continuance
of the advance that he sees now under way towards universal brotherhood will depend upon substitution of "the positive bond of mutual love" for calculations of expediency
and the deterrent force of mutual fear; but there is visible
evidence that another of his postulates, namely a working
harmony of the "higher religions," is moving from the range
of the possible to that of the probable.[6]

Reinhold Niebuhr sees no universal state above or on our
horizon. "Real historians," he tells us, are chary of prophecy
and cannot base prediction upon "generalizations about the
past."[7] He himself does not hesitate to make negative
prophecies. Thus he informs us that "the United Nations is

Die Atombombe und die Zukunft des Menschen (Chicago, 1961),
pp. 75, 81, 93, 97, 133, 142-159, 256.

[6] See *A Study of History* (London, 1948-61), 8: 215n; 9: 543-544;
12: 310, 531, 571; and *New York Times* Sunday Magazine, January
21, 1960, p. 60, and November 3, 1963, p. 23.

[7] H. B. Davis and R. C. Good, eds., *Reinhold Niebuhr on Politics*
(New York, 1960), pp. 46-47.

not, *and cannot be*, a constitutional world order,"[8] and later in the same volume that "the chaos of international relations *cannot be* overcome by any system of 'collective security.' "[9] The basic reason is stated in a third negative prediction to the effect that man is *"finally* 'unmanageable.' "[10]

In a somewhat less apocalyptic fashion, the Dutch sociologist, Bart Landheer, reaches conclusions similar to Niebuhr's. True, he believes that "world society" can be organized in such a way as to make it a working reality. But the organization, he holds, cannot be of the authoritative state type. Law in the traditional sense is appropriate to political society, but humanity has moved beyond that into an era of industrial society, where the principle of association is not coercive authority, but voluntary cooperation guided by "compromise rules, ethical principles, pragmatic behavioral rules, etc." The most likely structure would be one of regional security systems—for example, the United States and Western Europe, the Soviet Union and its satellites, the Arab states, Latin America, Africa—all functioning within the framework of the United Nations.

Yet, while he insists upon the voluntary character of most social activity in his world society, Landheer foresees a role, though a "relatively minor" one, for "coercive dispositions from above." In fact, he assigns to the Security Council, made up of "representatives of the security regions," an authority to make political decisions specifically in that most difficult terrain, disarmament, that most lawyers would unhesitatingly classify as legal in the traditional sense.[11] This exceeds any authority exercised by the present United Nations either in its Security Council or in its General Assembly.[12]

[8] *Nations and Empires* (London, 1960), p. 29. My emphasis.
[9] *Ibid.*, p. 194. My emphasis.
[10] *Ibid.*, p. 55-56. My emphasis.
[11] Bart Landheer, *On the Sociology of International Law and International Society* (The Hague, 1966), pp. 18, 54, 60-61, 76-77.
[12] Cf. un Charter, Art. 26.

13

Turning now from the philosophers, historians, and scientists to the legal profession, we find an explosion of interest and activity in the international field. For many centuries some lawyers, seeking to extend beyond national boundaries the conciliatory and pacifying operation of law, have participated in the elaboration and exposition of rules and principles to govern the conduct of states in their external relations. The conference diplomacy of the nineteenth century drew upon the profession for delegates, advisers, and draftsmen, while the revival of arbitration called for counsel and arbiters trained in law. From that time on, men with this kind of experience have joined with professors of international law to form such distinguished bodies as the Institute of International Law and the International Law Association, which have done great service in clarifying and expanding the formal norms of interstate behavior.

In the last four decades the legal staffs of foreign offices have multiplied in response to the demands of national relations with the new international agencies. Working for their several governments at the innumerable conferences that now provide some measure of international coordination and direction in most fields of human activity, they collaborate in drafting committees and confer with one another formally and informally, bringing to bear upon the problems of the agenda the dispassionate analysis which is their professional habit. There is less occasion in their councils for the vituperative antagonism that has deformed so much of the political debate between opponents in the cold war, and, though they cannot dictate, but only advise, they can at least sketch the rational lines of decisions that will come nearest to satisfying all participants. In bodies like the International Law Commission of the United Nations, lawyers often work out in advance the complex detail of solutions later adopted by diplomatic conferences. A comparison of the drafts submitted by such legal committees with

14

the texts finally adopted reveals how far this preliminary work goes toward shaping the ultimate agreement. In all this advisory and preliminary activity, invaluable assistance is rendered by the legal staffs permanently employed by the United Nations and related agencies.[13]

The men and women engaged in this specialized international work form a very small part of a very large profession, and until recently their work attracted little attention among lawyers in general. Now, however, relative indifference has given way to active collective concern. In 1952 the nongovernmental International Commission of Jurists began its work to promote the worldwide "rule of law" more particularly in its bearing upon human rights. Its "congresses of jurists" have brought together eminent lawyers from all the principal systems of law to study reports made by its research staff on violations of human rights in various countries and to formulate rules and principles for adoption and enforcement everywhere. What they seek is a unification of national laws to implement a community of human justice transcending states.

Since 1961 lawyers from more than a hundred states have joined in a campaign to strengthen international institutions to the point where they can ensure "world peace through law." Between June 1961 and April 1962, four continental conferences with this object were held on the initiative of a special committee of the American Bar Association. These meetings, quite unofficial in character, took place one after another in San José (Costa Rica), Tokyo, Lagos, and Rome. Following this broad-based preparation, a World Rule of Law Conference was convened in Athens in June 1963, and produced (after a preamble entitled "Proclamation of Athens," declaring that "law must replace force internationally as the controlling factor in the fate of humanity,"

[13] See report of Princeton Conference of Legal Advisers, 1963, in *Legal Advisers and Foreign Affairs* (Dobbs Ferry, N.Y., 1964).

and appealing to all peoples for support in translating this aspiration from "idea to reality") the following acta:

a) Declaration of General Principles for a World Rule of Law
b) Lawyers' Global Work Program to Advance a World Rule of Law
c) Resolutions Creating the World Peace through Law Center
d) Resolution to Prepare a Blueprint for Controlled Disarmament

No new truth will be found in these documents. The principles enunciated are all familiar. What is important—and it is very important—is the reiterated pledge of leading figures in the legal professions of more than a hundred countries to work for controlled disarmament, compulsory jurisdiction, and law enforcement, plus provision for a permanent institute and special committees to direct research and propaganda leading to these ends. The superb effort of the sponsors and managers of the five conferences has come as near as anything could to dedicating the membership of the world's bar and bench to the development of an effective legal order for mankind as a whole. The fusion of idealism and practical wisdom inspiring the program is indicated by the passages devoted to human rights and to the unification of private law, especially in the domain of international industry, trade, and finance. But the conferences themselves emphasized the rift that separates promise from performance in current world politics. Despite the general invitation, no participants came from Communist countries other than Yugoslavia.[14]

Readers of the reports of such conferences may well be left wondering how the lofty aims to which they so enthusi-

[14] Charles Rhyne, "The Athens Conference on World Peace Through Law," AJIL, 38 (1964), 138-51.

astically subscribe can be achieved short of a highly developed supranational government, and how many of the participants have pondered this question. The world federalists also include many excellent jurists, but no resolutions were passed commending their efforts. Some tribute might have been expected to such expertly elaborated plans as those of Grenville Clark and Louis B. Sohn in *World Peace Through World Law: Two Alternative Plans.*[15] But probably a majority of the participants would have agreed with Mr. E. P. Deutsch, Chairman of the American Bar Association's Committee on Peace and Law Through the United Nations, in his doubt whether such plans are not too remote from the realities of world politics to be adopted as a practical program.[16]

The doubt is justified. Soviet abhorrence of everything implying a reduction of the sovereignty of the USSR is fully shared by present-day France; and who can say how far the United States and the United Kingdom are prepared to go in subordinating themselves to supranational authority? Nor should anyone be misled by the impressive liberal movement that I have described into believing that a notoriously conservative profession has been wholly won over to the new outlook and activity. It would not be surprising, indeed, if a poll were taken, to find a majority still supporting the view that the state is the highest possible center of human authority.

The 1963 annual meeting of the American Society of International Law was enlivened by a discussion of the legality of the "quarantine" imposed upon Cuba by the United States in October of the previous year. That confrontation of the two Superpowers presented features of absorbing interest for international lawyers. Among these features was the fact that the naval measures announced in President

---

15 3rd ed. (Cambridge, Mass., 1966).
16 AJIL, 62 (1968), 229-30.

Kennedy's speech to the nation on the night of October 22 were set in motion before consultation with either the Organization of American States or the United Nations Security Council, though both bodies were informed before the hour when the stoppage of ships carrying arms to Cuba was actually to commence. Was the United States acting, then, as agent of the OAS, or merely using that regional organization to cover an act of national policy; and did the information conveyed to the Security Council and the failure of that body to take repressive action amount to the authorization of regional enforcement measures required by Article 53 of the United Nations Charter? Inadequate attention was, I think, paid to the possibility of a legal defense based upon *rebus sic stantibus*, on the argument, briefly mentioned in the President's speech, that the self-defense permitted by Article 51 of the Charter could no longer, since the invention of nuclear weapons, await actual attack. More perhaps might have been heard of this if former Secretary of State Dean Acheson had not intervened with a statement that limited law in its application to the state to a level that recalled Hegel.

Hegel had described the state as the absolute earthly power. Since international law depended upon completely autonomous wills, its formal imperatives represented moral aspirations rather than operative realities. Mr. Acheson declared that "much of what is known as international law is a body of ethical distillation" not to be confused with law. The issue raised by the "quarantine" was thus not a legal one. The Soviet challenge to the United States had raised questions of ultimate power upon which law had no bearing.[17]

Mr. Acheson dispenses with Hegel's metaphysical jargon;

[17] ASIL *Proceedings*, 1963, p. 14. Compare Hegel, *Grundlinien der Philosophie des Rechts*, trans. T. M. Knox as *Philosophy of Right* (Chicago, 1952), "Additions," paras. 330-331.

but his image of the state in action, as presented in the above passage, hardly differs from that of the historic champion of state absolutism. At a time when we hear so much about the welfare of the individual as the purpose of all political organization, it is wholesome to be reminded that a doctrine that makes the power of the state, envisaged not as a member of a community but as an entity standing by itself, the supreme consideration in international relations still prevails in government. But it would be far from wholesome to accept this condition of affairs as an immutable feature of civilization. In the circumstances now surrounding us, to do so would be to abandon hope for the future of man.

The danger of nuclear annihilation, which will always be with us so long as any state with the necessary resources is free to accumulate the weapons of mass destruction, bulks so large in most minds as to overshadow the other major problems which the present state system is incapable of solving. That may explain why there is as yet no international approach to these problems comparable even to the dawn of superpower cooperation for the restriction of atomic armaments.

The crisis of 1968 over the American balance of payments, with its onslaught on the dollar as an international reserve currency, emphasized the disastrous inadequacy of existing arrangements for financing international trade and development and the need for a supranationally controlled standard of currency and system of credit. The success of the International Monetary Fund, in its limited role of helping states over periods of depressed trade and weakening currency, has suggested that it should be endowed with the authority and means to make it an effective world reserve bank.[18]

[18] See e.g., Barbara Ward, *Spaceship Earth* (New York, 1968), esp. pp. 83, 89, 101-102.

The same agency might serve to regulate the flow of essential aid to the developing countries in their revolution of modernization, and even to mobilize much greater resources for the purpose. Unified supranational direction of this service would go far toward removing present suspicion of "neocolonial" design on the part of the lending states. As for the volume of aid, the present levels attained under national and international auspices are so far from adequate that the vast economic gap between the poverty-stricken "South" and the rich "North" steadily widens. In their insistent demand for development, the new nations of Africa and Asia form an arena of dangerous competition between Communist and democratic states in the purchase of political predominance. The overwhelming growth of their populations and their unsatisfied demand for a greater share in the world's wealth are in themselves a serious threat to general security. In the long run, peace is incompatible with such extremes of riches and poverty.[19]

It used to be an axiom of international discourse that with the growth of mutual knowledge and intercourse nations would settle their differences by the just and peaceful methods that legal systems are intended to provide. In fact, the peoples of the twentieth century, despite instantaneous communication and constant, swift interpenetration, still present a spectacle of conflict and disorder. Our mechanical intimacy has neither enthroned reason nor brought peace. The highlights of international relations seem the very antithesis of law. Never was there a time when faith in an ultimate world legal order seemed less in harmony with the behavior of governments and the course of events.

Is this an unalterable part of the nature of things? Can

[19] See Gunnar Myrdal, *Beyond the Welfare State* (New Haven, 1960), pp. 221-58; Escott Reid, *The Future of the World Bank* (Washington D.C., 1965); R. McNamara, *The Essence of Security* (New York, 1968); Barbara Ward, *op.cit.*

we reasonably expect anything deserving the name of law in an aggregate of units insisting upon sovereignty, refusing to be bound by any rule to which they have not given their individual consent, and unwilling to submit to overall government in the form of legislative and executive organs and courts of compulsory jurisdiction?

Certainly in such a milieu we cannot have what the once-revered English jurist, John Austin, termed law strictly and properly so called, that is to say, a body of commands addressed by a political superior to political inferiors and supported by sanctions penalizing disobedience. The international order, said Austin, amounts to nothing more than a moral code.

Yet, under the clamor of conflict that tends to monopolize popular attention, governments quietly carry on a vast amount of routine business with each other in accordance with established patterns, and make oral and written statements to the effect that these patterns constitute law binding upon states in the same way as national law is binding upon the citizen. The relations of states are by no means totally anarchic.

The appeal here, it should be noted, is to law, not to morals. Intergovernmental accusations of grossly immoral acts, of conduct contrary to "the dictates of the public conscience,"[20] answered sometimes by protestations of injured innocence, sometimes by mere *tu quoque*, are as common as changes in the weather. But the truth is that governments do not expect much of each other in the way of morals. Morality implies altruism, and for governments this is a peculiarly difficult virtue to practice. They are dedicated by their office to concentration upon the self-centered interests of the state to a degree that is commonly held to exempt the statesman in his public capacity from moral restraints that bear upon private action. Law is of course a

[20] Hague Conventions II, 1899; and IV, 1907, Preamble.

21

compound of morals and expediency, but it is mainly in this latter function that it is invoked in the relations of states. Certain principles like self-defense, exclusive jurisdiction in the national territory, freedom of the high seas, the binding effect of treaties, the immunity of heads of state and diplomatic missions, and nondiscrimination in the treatment of aliens, are judged essential to the survival and welfare of states. That is why they are invoked as law and not as mere standards of comity or righteousness. Violation of such principles is held to justify recourse to any competent international agency for protection or compensation, or, failing that, to reprisals.

Jurists anxious to secure for the existing international order general recognition as a system of the same genus as national law, find in these governmental communications and claims proof of their contention. There is, they argue, a general official conviction that the relations of states are subject to law in the strictest sense, therefore the law exists.[21] Austin's definition is an artificial and inadequate construction even of the highly integrated European orders that inspired it. True, the community of nations has no central legislative and executive authority, no courts of compulsory jurisdiction, no organized sanctions. But these, so the argument runs, are not essential elements of a legal system, since relatively well-observed public orders have existed, and in some primitive societies still exist, without some or any of them. The one indispensable thing—and the existence of this in the international community is held to be established by the communications mentioned above—is an underlying consensus that recognizes certain general community interests and endows them with precedence over individual claims. The rest is contingent detail. The main difference between the international and national

[21] Cf. H.L.A. Hart, *The Concept of Law* (Oxford, 1961), ch. 10, esp. pp. 225-26.

orders is that the former is a decentralized, or horizontal rather than vertical, order: that is to say, one in which the highest authority remains in the individual units of the community.[22]

This feat of abstract theory is not quite without practical merit. True, it evades the essential question that it is intended to answer, namely whether an order so decentralized, so horizontal, that it leaves to the subject the final decision as to what the law requires of him, can be assigned to the same class as those that impose objective decision. It does justice to the persistent official and unofficial effort of recent years to give form and substance to the concept of universal community, and to the usefulness of a weak normative order as a medium of communication for claims and counterclaims and a pattern of behavior in routine matters. The movement to convert this order into a vertical structure with a hierarchy of effective authority is far from universal, and where it is most active it is retarded by the grip of old doctrine, vested interests in the *status quo*, and confusion about the nature and extent of the changes that such a revolution in world politics must involve. But it has gained ground, and no excessive optimism is required to regard even the present stage as at least law in the making.

The Permanent Court of International Justice and its successor, the present International Court of Justice, may fairly be regarded as major steps in the development of a world legal system. Though the acceptance of jurisdiction remains optional—and this is a profound inferiority as compared with national courts—these tribunals have adjudicated a considerable number of disputes. The issues submitted have not been critically important in themselves, but they have furnished the occasion for permanently

[22] Cf. H. Kelsen, *General Theory of Law and State* (Cambridge, Mass., 1945), pp. 325-27; R. A. Falk, *Legal Order in a Violent World* (Princeton, 1968), pp. 77, 145, 147, and *passim*.

valuable clarifications of international rules. If the respect won in all but the Communist countries by the judgments and advisory opinions handed down at The Hague since 1922 resumes its growth after the setback of 1967 in the case of *Ethiopia and Liberia* v. *Republic of South Africa*, it must in time wear down resistance to the next step, which is compulsory jurisdiction.

In 1949 the International Court of Justice gave an advisory opinion that has a double claim to attention here. It illustrates the potential importance of findings by such a tribunal even on minor questions, and it asserts the possibility of supranational legislation even now. This opinion, which may come to be ranked as an historic breakthrough in international law, since it asserts the existence on the supranational plane of an essential institution of mature legal orders, was to the effect that "fifty States, representing the vast majority of the members of the international community [in 1945], had the power, in conformity with international law, to bring into being an entity [in this instance the United Nations] possessing objective international personality, and not merely personality recognized by them alone, together with capacity to bring international claims." This is a legislative act.

Is this finding authority for the proposition that any convention accepted by such a majority becomes law for all states? One way to approach an answer is to imagine that the proposition has been submitted to the General Assembly of the United Nations and to reckon the chances that it would receive the two-thirds majority vote required to make it a resolution of that body. This would of course be a mere test of consensus, since a General Assembly Resolution on such a matter has only the force of a recommendation. It seems improbable, given the strong resistance of the Soviet Union and its following, supported here by important Western states, to any proposal savoring of world government, that a draft resolution putting the question in this general and unambiguous form would pass.

For the purpose of further examination, however, let us assume that what the Court laid down is now an established general principle of international law and that a "vast majority of the members of the international community" can accordingly legislate for that whole community. We are left with the difficult question of what constitutes a "vast majority" in a community which has expanded from the sixty members of 1945 to the hundred and twenty-four of today. Suppose we adopt the two-thirds figure required for "decisions of the General Assembly on important questions" (Charter Art. 18.2) and now a frequent rule at international conferences. Follow through now to the conclusion that a convention thus supported would be law for all states, including the People's Republic of China with the world's largest population and Germany with its tremendous industrial power and military potential, neither of which would probably have been admitted to the proceedings. Here we pass the point where it ceases to make sense to draw out the logical implications of the most authoritative finding. Facts mock the syllogism.

Suppose then that we limit the legal effects to the participants in the conference and, abandoning the present practice that makes conventions binding only upon states that ratify, make them binding on all participants when a "vast majority" has ratified them. How many states would participate in conferences held under such a rule?

What the above examination suggests is that while the Court's advisory opinion asserts the present possibility of world legislation, it is far from presenting us with a workable legislative process. There is every reason to believe that we shall have to be content for an indefinite period with the crude substitute, essentially contractual rather than legislative, that limits the effects to states that become

25

parties to conventions by explicit acceptance. "Convention," the term constantly used for the products of multilateral conferences, means contract, not enactment, and is an accurate reflection of the present stage in the advance towards lawmaking on a universal scale.

What then of Article 2.6 of the Charter: "The Organization shall ensure that States which are not members of the United Nations act in accordance with these principles so far as may be necessary for the maintenance of international peace and security"? Is this to be taken as a bit of that objective lawmaking which the Court found in the creation of the United Nations as an international person, imposing obligations on nonconsenting states? Probably not. It need not be interpreted as anything more than an undertaking by the parties to the Charter to carry out competent decisions of the Organization even against states that have not become parties. There is no obligation on the part of nonmembers to submit. The clause does not make law for them.[23]

Imperfect as it is, the present cumbrous mode of proceeding toward world legislation by multilateral convention is capable of producing substantial results. The typical process is prolonged discussion and drafting by some such preparatory agency as the International Law Commission of the United Nations, followed by widely attended diplomatic conferences that recast the texts in the form of draft conventions for ratification by states represented at the conferences and accession by those not represented. Ratification or accession remains a voluntary act. Examples of important contributions made in this way to the developing law of nations are cited in other chapters.[24]

[23] L. M. Goodrich and E. Hambro, *Charter of the United Nations: Commentary and Documents* (Boston, 1946), p. 71; but see H. Kelsen, *The Law of the United Nations* (London, 1950), pp. 75-76, 106-10.

[24] See below, chs. 3 and 7.

When we remember the length and complexity of the debates that precede the enactment of important national statutes, the time taken to codify any portion of the law of nations ceases to be surprising. Every formula, apart from reconciling divergent interests, must survive the difficulties of equivalence in different languages and in different traditions of legal thought. The great conventions elaborated since 1947 are monuments of expert work that has not only formulated rules and principles for new problems but significantly reduced the uncertainty of some important areas in the existing international order. But no convention, however skillfully drafted, can remove the possibility of opposing interpretations in its application to specific situations. Among recent steps forward we must therefore record a highly constructive practice inaugurated under the League and continued under the United Nations. That is the inclusion in multilateral conventions of a clause obligating parties to submit to the World Court disputes about the meaning and application of the text. When this provision for authoritative interpretation is considered in conjunction with Article 94 of the Charter on measures to secure compliance with the Court's decisions, we can scarcely fail to recognize the seriousness of the official movement, with all its reservations and ambiguities, toward enlarging the role of law in the relations of states. Even the Soviet Union, than which no state is more insistent upon sovereignty, is a party to at least two conventions containing this clause.[25]

Reference to Article 94 of the Charter introduces another modest advance toward the normal structure of a legal system. The Covenant of the League of Nations (Art. 13.4) provided that "in the event of failure to carry out such an award or decision" (i.e., of an arbitral tribunal or the Permanent Court of International Justice) "the Council shall

[25] These are the Constitution of the ILO and the Revised Slavery Convention of 1956.

propose what steps should be taken to give effect thereto." Note the word "propose." There is no authority here to command or to carry out. Article 94 of the Charter is less timid. It stipulates that "if any party to a case fails to perform the obligations incumbent upon it under a judgment rendered by the Court, the other party may have recourse to the Security Council, which may, if it deems necessary, make recommendations or decide upon measures to be taken to give effect to the judgment." The effect of this is, briefly, that the United Nations has legal authority to enforce the Court's judgments. The Security Council need not act at all; it may merely recommend; or it may command. To recommend or command, it must have the vote of nine of its fifteen members including all five permanent members (Art. 27.3). This is a political decision, and if the losing litigant is itself a permanent member, or is in special favor with a permanent member, nothing stronger than a recommendation is probable, since a veto is likely to prevent a *decision* to enforce. In national legal orders, there are organs of the state legally bound to enforce judgments. The winning party claims this as of right, and there is no question of a political decision for or against enforcement. Here again the international legal system, if such we may call it, lags behind.

Taking full account of the ground gained since 1920, the fact remains that law is still far from playing the decisive role in determining the conduct of states that it plays in determining the conduct of the individual within the state. The underlying consensus does not go the length of that supporting national systems. Whatever governments and their apologists may say, self-preservation is always reserved, and in the international (unlike the national) sphere, self-preservation and the closely related self-defense are categories whose content, in the absence of explicit agreement to the contrary, is determined for all practical purposes by the party invoking them. A system in which pleas of self-preservation or self-defense are subject to authoritative scrutiny and abuses penalized, as they are in national law, differs as the day from night from one that provides no such objective control.

There is some truth but small comfort in the contention that international law is a primitive system. This is merely a restatement of our problem. The international order is indeed like primitive systems in its lack of organs of special and authoritative competence, but unlike them in its inefficacy at critical points. Primitive systems are adapted to primitive conditions. Among the nations of the modern world, relations become as multifarious, complex, and sensitive as those among citizens of the state, and demand delicately adapted modes of regulation. There is no bond in this congeries of quarrelsome units remotely approaching the absorption of the individual in his tribe, a completeness of psychophysical identification that explains the efficacy of diffuse pressures to conform. The level of law observance reached in primitive societies can only be attained here through powerful agencies with clear-cut functions. Our nearest approach to the necessary mechanism is the Security Council of the United Nations with its Military Staff Committee; and conflicts of interest among the Great Powers, provoking the veto, have robbed that organ of the strength which the Charter ostensibly intended it to possess. As for a standing parliament of man to keep the letter and machinery of the law adapted to the rapid developments of our world, everything suggests that the day for that is far distant.

It may be that general submission to adjudication is the least remote of the changes needed to strengthen the world rule of law. Powerful influences in the United States urge the withdrawal of the stultifying reservation of domestic jurisdiction as defined by the United States, and such a lead

29

towards genuine acceptance of the jurisdiction of the International Court of Justice would almost certainly stimulate a wider movement in the same direction. Here the Soviet Union remains the great question mark. Never yet has it submitted to adjudication by this tribunal, and save in commercial matters its acceptances of other modes of non-Soviet adjudication or arbitration have been negligible.[26] It clings to the doctrine that between Communism and capitalism no impartial adjudication is possible even if it were desirable. To expect a change in this position is to expect a shift in Soviet policy away from the fanatical promotion of Communism as the one acceptable mode of social existence and toward tolerance of other modes, such as capitalism. This will have to await recognition, not only by the Communist but also by the Western Powers, of a wider range of common interests that take precedence over diverse theories and modes of social, economic, and political organization.

An international legal order without compulsory jurisdiction comes very close to being a contradiction in terms. The need is particularly acute in an aggregate that has not reached the stage of integration marked by parliamentary institutions, for here we are without an essential part of the normal mechanism for discovering and recording that consensus which is conceded to be the essential basis of law. *One part*; for even the best legislative organ is never wholly adequate to this purpose. It must be supplemented by courts with final authority to decide the disputes that arise about the meaning of the most carefully drawn enactments and to declare the content of consensus where the codes are silent. In the international sphere, where codification by convention has left such wide areas uncharted, the content of the consensus embodied in custom is open to literally in-

[26] See J. F. Triska and R. M. Slusser, *The Theory, Law and Policy of Soviet Treaties* (Stanford, 1962), pp. 353-55, 381-88.

terminable argument, with each contestant entitled to equal respect for his version.

Three currently important examples will serve to prove the point. One is the width of the territorial sea; another, the standard of justice measuring the responsibility of states for injuries to aliens; and a third, the compensation due on expropriation of alien property.[27]

What, it is asked, could a supranational court of final appeal do in matters such as these, where prolonged negotiation and legal argument have failed to produce agreement? It would give an authoritative answer to the question whether any claim is supported by a consensus. This, it is true, might not settle the dispute, but merely shift it from the legal to the political arena, since, as we have seen, the international machinery for the enforcement of judicial decisions is still, in spite of Article 94 of the Charter, weak and uncertain. But it would at least show where the existing law stands on the specific issue. This would enable all interested parties to adjust their activities accordingly, or, if they regard the rule as obsolete, to set in motion a drive for its modification or replacement by convention. This kind of interaction between adjudication and legislation is a commonplace of national government. In a fitful way, the voluntary use of arbitration and adjudication on the international plane helps to direct the planning and work of "lawmaking" conferences. A judicial hierarchy of regional and universal courts with compulsory jurisdiction would substitute regularity and consistency for the haphazard operation of existing institutions. There is no other definitive way of clearing up uncertainties in the law whether *before or after* codification.

The object of the next two chapters is a general evalua-

[27] For a recent official statement of the US law on the last mentioned question, see State Dept. release on Ceylon's 1962-63 expropriations, AJIL, 58 (1964), 168-69.

tion of the body of norms known as public international law. This, with all its weaknesses, records the most sustained advance towards a planetary legal system. Because the end of the Second World War was also the beginning of the atomic age, when dangers unprecedented in their nature and scope have stimulated new energy in the official and unofficial search for effective means to control international violence, the year 1945 has been taken as the dividing line between two distinct periods of growth.

In the first, long, period, the states participating in the formation of international law and formally entitled to its benefits were mostly those of Europe or of European culture, and numbered hardly more than sixty. Since 1945, all cultures have been represented in the process of development and codification; the total of participating states has passed one hundred and twenty-five; and the area of application encompasses not only our planet but outer space as well. It is a new era.

2.

PUBLIC INTERNATIONAL LAW BEFORE 1945

T HE international law that is invoked in the relations of all states today got its systematic formulation largely in Europe. Patterns of practice relating to such matters as the beginning and conduct of hostilities, embassies, treaties, and maritime commerce had been inherited from remote ages and regions. A flood of European juristic literature beginning in the sixteenth century poured into this nucleus ingredients from the Roman civil-law texts and from natural law, blending the mixture with an infusion of legal theory and strengthening it with legendary or historical episodes in the relations of princes.

The body of juristic materials so composed might, it was hoped, govern or at least guide the rulers of the nation-states that were reassembling the feudal fragments of power and repudiating even the theoretical and formal authority of the Holy Roman Empire. The conception of human community entertained by the Greek Stoics and transmitted through their Roman successors to medieval Christendom had been submerged under the concentration of power in these separate entities, each of which asserted absolute authority in its own domain, demanded the ultimate devotion of its subjects, and determined finally its relations with the rest. This individualistic structure of the state system has proved durable enough to withstand all the forces making for transnational community. It still constitutes the basic assumption shaping the conduct of governments when interests that they deem vital are at stake.

33

The fund of precept and example called law of nations or, after Jeremy Bentham, international law, was of course unenforced, since there was no human authority superior to states. Nor was it generally subject to objective interpretation and application, since there was no standing international judicature, and submission to arbitration was by no means frequent. It was the book of the rules for a game played without umpires.

The great stimulus in the formulation of these rules was war. The important questions for the early writers had been, first, the kind of injury suffered or anticipated that justified recourse to war, and then the kind of acts that rendered illegal a war legally begun. As late as the seventeenth century—the age of Suarez, Grotius, and Pufendorf—the law of peace was a secondary study; it was an examination of the rights and duties whose actual or threatened violation made recourse to war legal. Not until the end of the eighteenth century did the attempt to establish something more than a moral distinction between *bellum justum* and *bellum injustum* disappear from the prevailing doctrine. In the next hundred years the growth of positivism, with its sharp distinction between moral precept and legal rule, though it by no means closed the gap between the legal literature and the accepted practice of states, at least began to narrow it. A rule calling for legal judgment upon the reasons that induced states to go to war entailed an encroachment upon the sovereignty considered to be their fundamental right. So, while the demand for some mitigation of the slaughter, destruction, and general dislocation of war had grown to a strength that called for official action to supplement the traditional literary exhortation, the response was an attempt not to outlaw war, but to limit its methods and weapons.

The resulting nineteenth-century intergovernmental conferences marked a shift in importance from juristic writings to diplomatic negotiation in the elaboration of rules. The Declaration of Paris, 1856, resolved a number of disputed points touching contraband and blockade. The Geneva Convention of 1864 establishing the Red Cross, and regulating the treatment of sick and wounded in the field, has proved one of the great humanitarian achievements of modern times. In 1868 the Declaration of St. Petersburg condemned the use of explosive bullets as an unnecessary cruelty. Six years later fourteen states drew up at Brussels a code of eighty-six articles on the laws and customs of land warfare. This failed ratification, but provided much of the material for the Hague Conventions of 1899.

Preoccupation with war and the hope of reducing its savagery by prohibiting certain types of weapons and practices was again emphasized in the misnamed Hague Peace Conferences of 1899 and 1907. Initiated by Nicholas II of Russia with the announced purpose of promoting peaceful settlement and preparing the way for reduction of armaments, these meetings, though their main product was rules of war, did produce codes of procedure for good offices, mediation, inquiry, and arbitration. They also provided for a panel of arbiters from which states might constitute a tribunal if they saw fit to use this mode of ending a dispute. Though it never sits and has no jurisdiction, this body of jurists rejoices in the name "Permanent Court of Arbitration." At the Conference of 1907 the United States pressed for a real standing court with a bench of fulltime judges; but no mode of manning such a bench that would satisfy both great and small states could be devised at that time. A plan was drawn up for an International Court of Prize. Differences on many points of the law regarding relations between belligerents and neutrals caused the postponement of this project pending elaboration of a code. This was attempted in London in the winter of 1908-09, but the elaborate declaration drawn up by that Conference was rejected by the host state, still the greatest naval power, and, except for a tentative period in the war of 1914-18, was never brought into force. One useful contribution to peace made by the Hague Conference of 1907 was the convention embodying Dr. Drago's proposal to limit the use of force for the recovery of international contract debts. The striking fact, however, is that of the fourteen draft conventions adopted by that Peace Conference, twelve were concerned with war.

The governments meeting at The Hague (twenty-six in 1899 and forty-four in 1907) acted on the belief that war is a natural and inevitable expression of human nature. Any notion that it might be superseded as a way of settling the graver sorts of international conflict was too remotely idealistic to figure prominently or steadily in the formation of official policy. Various devices such as mediation, good offices, arbitration, even a rule stipulating a declaration or ultimatum before opening hostilities, might reduce the frequency of this resort to force, and the prohibition of excessively destructive implements and modes of attack might temper its inevitable cruelty. But war was a permanent social institution, an accepted mode of promoting or defending national interests. The Hague Conferences did nothing to alter the prevailing official doctrine that every sovereign state was legally free to use war as an instrument of national policy irrespective of the justice of its demands. If the paradox of invoking a law of international conduct and yet admitting that any situation could be legally altered by force was perceived, it apparently disturbed neither the official reason nor the official conscience. Nor did the writers on international law boggle at the contradiction.

The First World War shook this complacency. Upon many commanders and in many situations the painfully elaborated laws of war acted as a moderating influence. They were also atrociously broken. Not only were there barbarities on the battlefield, on the high seas, and in the treatment of civilian populations, but the customary and conventional norms designed to keep war from spreading and to preserve areas of normal activity for states not engaged in the hostilities were overridden by hard-pressed belligerents desperately anxious to prevent their enemies from getting any kind of supplies or services from neutrals. The doctrine of legal reprisals for an opponent's illegalities was stretched to justify measures that penalized states whose only offense had been inability to enforce their neutrality against powerful belligerents. Self-preservation excused actions that shocked all conscience. Neither the humane literature of international law nor the accumulation of official conventions could keep belligerent operations within pre-established limits. Demonstrably, war could not be kept clean.

In itself, the demonstration would probably not have been enough to bring about the change of direction in the development of international law that now occurred. The necessary additional impetus came from the growing conviction that war from now on would impose an intolerable burden of suffering and loss. It was no longer a clash of armies but an all-absorbing battle of whole peoples. The indiscriminately destructive power of new weapons, to say nothing of the proven or imagined horrors of chemical and bacteriological warfare, had generated an irresistible demand for official international action not to mitigate but to prevent war. Henceforward, the main thrust was to be in the direction of imposing pacific settlement of conflict through the application of a clarified and progressively codified law of nations. International organization and the development of international law were now to proceed hand in hand.

The Covenant of the League of Nations could not yet quite "outlaw" war. To the statesmen gathered at Versailles, a superstate was not only a sacrilegious phantasy; it was a threat to the high personal authority that they derived from manipulation of the sovereign prerogatives of the national state. What the Covenant did was merely to create a standing organization which, it was hoped, in addition to bringing pressure upon states for the peaceful solution of existing conflicts, would by its political, economic, and social activities remove some of the underlying causes of war. On the assumption that, in spite of any possible preventive measures, wars would still occur, some effort was still directed to mitigating their savagery. Thus the London Protocol of 1936, to which forty-two states, including all the great naval powers, were parties, required submarine commanders to provide for the safety of passengers and crew before sinking merchant vessels that did not resist visit and search. Gas warfare was prohibited in various treaties and in a Protocol of 1925, in which again more than forty states participated. In 1923 a Commission of Jurists, appointed under the Washington Disarmament Treaty of the previous year, drew up at The Hague an elaborate code on warfare in the air. This never came into force for want of ratification. In 1929 the series of conventions on the care of the wounded and on the treatment of prisoners of war was revised and improved.

From 1919 on, the emphasis in international planning was nevertheless not on the regulation of war, but on its prevention. This was the rationale of ten years of laborious negotiation on disarmament. At first the prospect looked bright. The Washington Conference of 1921-22 brought about the scrapping of some British, American, and Japanese battleships, and temporarily suspended building in the battleship class. It also limited battleship tonnage for Japan, France, and Italy to 60, 35, and 35 percent respectively of the equalized British and American tonnage. In 1934, however, Japan, well launched upon her program of dominance

in the Far East, denounced the Washington Treaty and resumed large-scale naval building.

Even such temporary success as that of the Washington
Conference was denied the League of Nations in its attempt at general disarmament. Prominent in the Covenant
(Art. 8) was the finding that the arms race, the desperate
effort to ensure superiority in anticipated wars, was itself
a cause of war. "The members of the League recognize that
the maintenance of peace requires the reduction of national
armaments to the lowest point consistent with national
safety and the enforcement by common action of international obligations." The Council of the League, assisted by
a Permanent Commission, was given the task of planning
for this reduction, and the work went on until 1933 when,
amid gathering storms, the Disarmament Conference, convened in the previous year, adjourned *sine die*. The Conference, despite years of technical preparation, had been unable to agree upon equivalences of weapons systems or of
effectives and reserves, or to solve the problem of reconciling Germany's insistence upon equality with France's demand for security. French proposals to impose compulsory
arbitration, and to place at the disposal of the League military forces strong enough to prevent aggression, went far
beyond any European commitment that either Great
Britain or the United States was prepared to make. It had
been found impossible, in other words, to reach agreement
upon either the necessary abstract rules or the structure for
their enforcement. As we shall see, these same problems
still, after a Second World War and two more decades of
arms-length negotiation, defy solution.

Other attempts had been made to meet the security demands of France and other neighbors of Germany. One
had taken form in the Geneva Protocol of 1924, which set
out to close the gap in the Covenant that permitted states
to avoid adjudication or arbitration and ultimately to re-

sort to force. Unanimously and enthusiastically approved by an assembly led by Aristide Briand of France and Britain's Labor Prime Minister, Ramsay MacDonald, this would have provided the sinews of a much stronger legal order. It was coldly scrapped by the Conservative government which soon took over power in London and whose fears of implication in punitive or preventive action that might lead to embroilment with the United States were shared by Canada and other Dominions. The Locarno Treaties of 1925, with their guarantees of German and French frontiers, were a partial and temporary substitute destined to be swept away by the failure of the Disarmament Conference and Hitler's rise to power.

Two events in 1928 were believed at the time to mark a substantial advance toward world order. These were the Briand-Kellogg Pact, alias Pact of Paris, and the General Act for Pacific Settlement. The first, which was ratified by no less than sixty-five states, including the United States and the Soviet Union, purported to be a renunciation of war as an instrument of national policy and an undertaking never to seek by other than peaceful means the settlement of any dispute. Even the theoretical effect of this was largely annihilated by an unstated but firmly understood exception of the subjectively determined and therefore uncontrollable right of self-defense. As for any practical consequence, the Pact stands as a monument to the frailty of verbal undertakings unsupported by organized power. The same can be said of the Argentine Anti-War Treaty of 1933, which added a clause declaring the intention of the parties never to recognize territorial acquisitions made by force of arms. The General Act, adopted by the League Assembly within a month of the signature of the Paris Pact, was designed to complement it by creating a positive obligation of pacific settlement and by defining the modes of settlement (conciliation, arbitration, or submission to the Permanent Court of International Justice) when traditional diplomacy failed. This was much too rigorous and precise for either the Soviet Union or the United States, and their abstention doubtless goes some way to explain the fact that only a minority of states, twenty-three in all, ever ratified the General Act. An even greater lack of enthusiasm attended the revision of this instrument in 1949. The revision was stoutly resisted by the Soviet Union, which saw in it nothing more or less than a conspiracy to defeat the veto by taking international conflicts out of the hands of the Security Council. Only six states, Belgium, Sweden, Norway, Denmark, Luxembourg, and Upper Volta had accepted the revised agreement by the end of 1967, eighteen years after its drafting.[1]

The Committee of Jurists appointed by the first Assembly of the League of Nations to complete the draft statute for the Permanent Court of International Justice took a serious view of the common excuse for refusing to submit to arbitration, namely the uncertainties of international law. It proposed codification as the remedy. The Committee seems to have passed rather lightly over the fact that uncertainties as to the validity and meaning of domestic norms, whether customary or legislative, are a commonplace in the administration of national justice, and that the one way yet discovered to end them is to establish courts with the compulsory authority of interpretation. When meaning is not clear, what was the legislative consensus, or what is the consensus of the community? Courts are an indispensable means of answering such questions with finality. When, therefore, states refuse to submit to arbitration or adjudication, they prevent the removal of the uncertainties of which they complain. Codification can indeed help to clarify; but it is no final solution, since verbal formulas, however carefully

---

[1] See UN, *Multilateral Treaties in respect of which the Secretary-General performs Depository Functions, list of ratifications, accessions, etc. as at December 31, 1967*, p. 29.

elaborated, are notoriously uncertain in their application to specific situations.

International codification, nevertheless, like national legislation, is one step in the ascertainment and formulation of consensus, and its importance increases as a long-established group of states is swollen by new members who have had next to nothing to do with the development of existing norms. It was well, therefore, that the League should have set out upon a course that has proved long, tortuous, and laborious.

For six years, the committees set up by the League discussed points of difference, drafted texts, addressed questionnaires to governments, and considered the statements of national position so elicited. Finally, three subjects were chosen as "ripe for codification" and placed on the agenda of the Hague Codification Conference of 1930. These were nationality, the territorial sea, and the responsibility of states for injuries to the persons or property of aliens.

The prime object in all the work done on nationality was to reduce the frequency of both statelessness and double nationality, and, where these would still occur, to alleviate the resulting hardships. With all their professed devotion to the welfare of their citizens, there are still governments that not only wall them in and shoot them if they attempt to escape, but deprive them of nationality for some offenses and leave them to the tender mercies of any state that they contrive to enter. The stateless person is without diplomatic or consular protection; he has no travel documents unless he can obtain a Nansen passport or its equivalent from an international refugee agency; a home and employment may be waiting for him in a country to which he cannot gain admission. The state of origin is as yet under no general obligation either to permit expatriation or to readmit a former national rendered stateless by its decree. The person with two nationalities is not in such bad case; but his obligations to different states may involve heavy penalties.

The sole convention that the Hague Conference of 1930 produced was a gallant attempt to establish the humane principle stated in its preamble that "every person should have a nationality and should have one nationality only." Another good product was the Protocol exempting persons with double nationality from military obligations except in the country where they reside. Unfortunately each of these instruments was ratified by only eleven states, and the struggle for the general principle has been inherited by the United Nations.

The committee of the Hague Conference to which the topic of state responsibility was assigned drafted and adopted a number of articles on specific points, but broke down on the fundamental question of the standard of treatment due to aliens. An unexpectedly large minority (seventeen out of thirty-eight votes) held that the alien was entitled only to equal treatment with nationals, while the majority (twenty-one) insisted that the state must observe a minimum international standard. The Conference accordingly failed to achieve either convention or protocol.

A similar fate attended the effort to conclude a convention on the territorial sea, though the Conference was able to append to its Final Act thirteen provisionally approved articles "with a view to their possible incorporation in a general convention on the territorial sea." That this was not a vain hope will be clear to anyone comparing the text with the Convention on the Territorial Sea and Contiguous Zone concluded at Geneva in 1958. Again the drive for a convention was stopped by failure to agree upon a fundamental question. How wide is the marginal belt subject to national sovereignty, and are states entitled to exercise limited powers in a contiguous zone beyond this? At Geneva in 1958 the

43

conference bypassed the first point, and a second conference in 1960 failed to reach agreement upon it. The 1958 Convention did, however, recognize special rights in a contiguous zone not exceeding twelve miles from the baseline from which territorial waters are measured. This has the effect of putting an outer limit of twelve miles on the authority of the riparian state, though, with the exception of the Soviet Union, the greatest maritime Powers still cling to the principle that territorial sovereignty in the full sense ends three miles from the coastal baseline.

It is putting it mildly to say that the meager formal product of the Hague Conference of 1930 was a disappointment to international lawyers. On the other hand, the documentary interchange with governments—questions and answers on points under discussion—the reports of the expert committee, and the great series of studies dedicated by the Harvard Research to the advancement of the codification project, are a treasure house for the student and an invaluable aid to those engaged, thirty years later, in the collective endeavor to promote "the progressive development of international law and its codification."[2]

Here, as in many other fields, the League of Nations laid the groundwork of method and experience in an essential world service upon which the successor organization has been able to build. But no record of the League's contribution to the development and codification of international law should end with an enumeration of secondary and delayed results. Multilateral conventions of immediate utility were drawn up at conferences which, though not part of the specific program of codification, were held under the auspices of the League or associated organizations. One notable example is the series that began at Barcelona in 1921 with the Conventions on Freedom of Transit and the Regime of International Waterways. Another is the pair of

[2] See UN Charter, Art. 13.1a.

Geneva Conventions, dated 1925 and 1931, that brought new vigor into the effort, initiated at The Hague in 1912, to control the international traffic in opium and other narcotic drugs. Most prolific of all was the International Labor Organization, whose monumental output of conventions and recommendations has had a major part in fashioning contemporary social legislation.

No less important for the growth of world law was the Statute of the Permanent Court of International Justice drawn up, under Article 14 of the Covenant, at the first session of the League's Assembly. This enactment, solving problems that had defeated the Hague Peace Conference of 1907, defined the constitution and powers of the first standing tribunal open to all states. Adopted almost without change as the constituent instrument of the International Court of Justice, "the principal judicial organ of the United Nations," in 1969 it numbered 129 parties, that is to say all states members of the United Nations plus Switzerland, Liechtenstein, and San Marino.

The evasive recalcitrance of states prevented this court, as it has prevented the United Nations tribunal, from becoming the great agency of pacific settlement that the champions of international adjudication had hoped. It was never allowed to decide major issues of international conflict. But the importance of its work is not to be finally measured by the gravity of the disputes submitted to it. Legal precedents of lasting significance may be established in the adjudication of cases where the immediate stake is small, and the judgments and advisory opinions of the Permanent Court of International Justice, while not formally binding upon that or any other tribunal (Article 59 of the Statute), stand today among the most authoritative statements of the law of nations. The validity and limits of the restrictive interpretation of international instruments, as propounded in "The Wimbledon" (PCIJ Series A, No. 1);

the changing content of domestic jurisdiction (Tunis and Morocco Nationality Decrees, PCIJ Series B, No. 4); the creation of rights in individuals by international agreements (Danzig Railway Officials, PCIJ Series B, No. 15); the relative degrees of control required in *occupatio* (Eastern Greenland, PCIJ Series A/B, No. 53)—these are only a few of the matters in which this creation of the League proved its seminal role. Its reports are the first volumes of a sustained and systematic international case law.[3]

[3] See e.g., M. O. Hudson, *The Permanent Court of International Justice, 1920-1942* (New York, 1943); H. Lauterpacht, *The Development of International Law by the International Court of Justice* (London, 1958); E. Hambro, *The Case Law of the International Court of Justice* (Leyden, 1952).

3.

PUBLIC INTERNATIONAL LAW SINCE 1945

IN the last thirty years the study and the development of international law have been enriched by the new and intensive analysis of international relations. Whether or not the recent prominence of this study justifies its classification as a distinct discipline, there is no doubt that it has focused upon the interaction of states some of the best talent in psychology, sociology, anthropology, political science, and jurisprudence. This has meant research in depth into human conduct as it is affected by political, social, and economic organization, into the causes and resolution of conflict, into the bases and operation of power, and into the divergence and convergence of power and law.

Among specialists in international law, manifestations of the new trend may be found in the very general rejection of nineteenth-century positivism, with its insistence upon the consent of states, its sharp distinction between law and morals, and its emphasis upon state sovereignty as the basic principle of the international legal order. Hans Kelsen was among the earliest to abandon the consent of states as the formal source of binding international norms. In place of Jellinek's autolimitation, he propounded the doctrine of the *Grundnorm*, which he ultimately formulated for the international legal system as "states must behave as they have customarily behaved." Every norm that could be traced back to this postulate, and no other, was a rule of international law. Kelsen's most distinguished student, Sir Hersch

Lauterpacht, preferred as *Grundnorm* "the will of the international community must be obeyed."

As the basis of every legal system Kelsen and his pure-science-of-law school found such a fundamental hypothesis, formulated, for municipal systems, as "Whatever the founding fathers have decreed, and everything decreed in conformity with the constitutional norms adopted by them, and nothing else, is law." But Kelsen's was a unitary approach to law, and in his theory every legal system was ultimately derived from the same basic postulate. This left two choices—either all national systems must be traced back to the international *Grundnorm*, or the international system must find its authority in the national *Grundnorm*. This was the choice between international monism, which gave primacy to the international order and made all national orders derivations of the international, and state monism, which made the international order a derivative of the national. Kelsen asserted a scientific indifference, though not a moral or political indifference, as between international and state monism; but contemporary jurisprudence for the most part deplores this indifference and posits the limitation of state sovereignty by international law. But again for the most part, and with doubtful consistency, it describes the international legal order as one of coordination, not of superordination, or, metaphorically, as a horizontal rather than a vertical order. This doctrine harks back to Kelsen's thesis that the international order is one of decentralized authority, the decision-makers being state governments rather than supranational officials. But since the authority to decide is itself a product of law, this position would appear to involve acceptance of state primacy.

In its rejection of Kelsen's "neo-positivism," prevalent doctrine now especially condemns his scientific indifference to the moral content of legal rules. Yet its concessions to power in the application of these rules are not easily dis-

tinguishable from moral indifference. Balancing these concessions is a frankly teleological approach to the solution
of legal problems, where the end result in its bearing on
human values is given a weight it could not have in Kelsen's insistence upon the discovery and strict application of
a pre-established rule.[1]

The influence of the new jurisprudence is visible both in
the codifying work of the United Nations' International
Law Commission and in that of the International Court of
Justice. The International Law Commission's discovery and
avowal of the impossibility of any clear-cut separation between codification and development bears a close relationship to the Court's obscuring of the traditionally sharp formal distinction between adjudication and legislation in such
decisions as those on the reparation of injuries suffered in
the service of the United Nations and the Anglo-Norwegian
fisheries. In these three instances the recent more flexible
and more teleological type of legal thought triumphed.
That the more rigid school still flourishes, however, is attested in the casting vote that determined the judgment on
the merits in the case of Ethiopia and Liberia versus the
Republic of South Africa.

The interaction of jurisprudence, the Court's decisions,
and the Law Commission's drafts is inevitable. The Court's
bench and the Commission's membership have regularly included many of the most distinguished jurists of our time.

[1] See Hans Kelsen, *General Theory of Law and State*, trans.
A. Wedberg (Cambridge, Mass., 1949), and *Principles of International
Law*, rev. and ed. Robert W. Tucker, 2nd ed. (New York, 1966);
G. Schwarzenberger, *Manual of International Law*, 5th ed. (New
York, 1967); and *The Inductive Approach to International Law* (Lon-
don and Dobbs Ferry, N.Y., 1965); Charles De Visscher, *Theory and
Reality in Public International Law*, trans. Percy E. Corbett, rev. ed.
(Princeton, 1968); M. S. McDougal and F. P. Feliciano, *Law and
Minimum World Public Order* (New Haven, 1961); and, for an
invaluable summary, the four volumes of Richard A. Falk and Saul
H. Mendlovitz, eds., *The Strategy of World Order* (New York, 1966).

If there is among them one dominant doctrine as to the nature of the international normative order, I should say that it classifies that order as a legal system, but a primitive one. If "primitive" here refers to the law of primitive societies, we must admit that primitive law had a completeness and an effectiveness that our international order lacks. If pressed to identify the basis of the rules said to be binding upon states, some would say, along with H.L.A. Hart, that international law exists because governments believe it does.[2] This, like the description "primitive," glosses over the important fact that governments consider themselves bound only by what they choose to regard as law, and even so, assert the existence of vital interests that are beyond the reach of law. This means that the "system" leaves off precisely at the point where law is most necessary, namely where the urge to unrestrained action is strongest. Such subjectivity and inadequacy are alien to primitive systems.

Decentralization, coordination rather than superordination, horizontal rather than vertical structure, primitiveness —all these theses and metaphors serve as apologies for the obvious weaknesses of a normative order whose title to classification as a legal system is an eternally debatable question of semantics.

If "primitive" meant only that the system is at an early stage of development, the description would be nearer the truth. After all, the Roman system in the far-from-primitive republican stage still had features of the present international order, such as the absence of official machinery to bring a defendant before the magistrate and the failure to provide effective means of enforcing judgments.

It is my contention that we can dispense with apology and metaphor if we are content to regard the international normative order as a world legal system in the making rather than one that is already made, where the recourse

[2] *The Concept of Law* (Oxford, 1961), p. 226.

to violent self-help has not been decisively limited by the combination of accepted formal definition and collective control that now characterizes municipal law.

There are pessimistic strains in contemporary international legal theory, leading, in some writers, to a fatalistic acceptance of the view that man has reached, in the sovereign state, the limit of his political potentialities. Some of the best intellects in the field, discounting his vast historical progress in government under law, adopt a tone verging on the scornful when they analyze his stumbling, ambivalent essays in supranational organization and legislation. In this they display a lack of perspective no less real than that of the hurried idealists whose visions they deprecate.

Article 13 of the United Nations Charter instructs the General Assembly to "initiate studies and make recommendations for the purpose of: . . . encouraging the progressive development of international law and its codification." Acting under this Article and Article 22, the General Assembly created the International Law Commission as its principal subsidiary organ to assist in this task; but a number of other bodies acting under the Assembly's authority have also drafted conventions and declarations that have an important place in the program of development and codification. We shall later have occasion to examine these products in some detail. What concerns us for the moment is the general conduct and fortunes of the program as a whole.

From the beginning this effort to clarify and fill out the prescriptions and procedures of a world order responsive to present and predictable needs had to contend with all the contradictions, ambivalences, and antagonisms that beset the structural side of the enterprise. National sovereignty, always on the alert to fend off any threat of diminution, found its most resolute champion in the Soviet Union, with the United States, Britain, and France not far behind. The division of the world into competing power blocs, aggravated, if not caused, by the conflict of ideologies, made the International Law Commission a forum for political polemics, a distortion undeterred by the fact that its members were supposed to be independent experts rather than representatives of governments. The same was true of the officially manned Commission on Human Rights as it drafted the covenants designed to transform the 1948 Declaration into treaty law. Since the détente of 1953, the proceedings of the International Law Commission have shown some improvement in tone and in results—a change that again manifests the influence of political contingencies on the work of international bodies even when the assigned function is one of technical expertise.

In every milieu, of course, legislative programs must battle their way through conflicts of sectional and group interests and of political doctrine. The important difference between the national and international arenas is that in the latter the reconciling sense of community is relatively weak and the lawmaking end-product is usually binding only upon such units as accept it. The now normal provision for majority decision in the specialized international agencies is a step towards more effective structure, though here again the formal sovereignty of the state is preserved by the liberty to withdraw.

There is reason to believe that some of the obstacles created by Marxist political theory to Communist-capitalist cooperation in the development of international law are diminishing. Soviet jurists appear to have abandoned early debates about the possibility and the nature of a general law of nations. They still insist upon the invariable superiority of the socialist international law which they describe as operating among the Communist countries and to which they predict that all the world will eventually rally. Pending this consummation, however, they are prepared to recognize a system "expressing the will of the ruling classes" and binding upon all states regardless of social theory and structure. This contrived formula makes it possible for them to assert the existence of international law without quite deserting Marx's definition of law as a means adopted by the dominant class in all societies to control and exploit the subject strata. They find further comfort in attributing all enrichments of the general system to importations from the socialist code.

Reconciling Soviet doctrine to the existence of general international law there was finally the conception that this, being like other laws an instrument of politics, could be used as a weapon against opposing states. The relation of this theory to the Marxist notion of law as a tool by which a dominant class controls subordinate classes in its own interest is fairly clear. In a speech published in *Pravda* on November 25, 1948, the redoubtable A. Y. Vyshinski announced that "Law in general is nothing but an instrument of politics," and this, rather than an objective binding order, was the image of international law emphasized in the Soviet legal literature until 1956, when G. I. Tunkin thought a correction necessary. If the statement that international law is an instrument of politics meant nothing more than that states, like individuals within the state, invoke law to support their claims, it would be a harmless truism. But the emphasis given it by Vyshinski and his followers suggested that states, being subject to no universal authority empowered to interpret international law, might read into it such meaning as served their purposes, subject only to any moral scruples felt by their rulers. Such a conception, to which the practice of states has unhappily lent much support, would of course rob the norms of international conduct of all distinctive legal character. Tunkin, in an article in *Sovietskoe Gosudarstvo i Pravo*,[3] takes the position that in-

[3] 1956, no. 7, p. 11.

ternational law, "besides being a fund of principles and norms binding upon all states, is, like all law, an instrument of policy, and is so used in some measure by socialist and capitalist states in execution of their foreign policy"; but he adds the important qualification that it can only be so used within limits set by the norms themselves.[4] This brings us back to the harmless truism, and to an image of international law which it is to be hoped will be accepted not only in the Soviet Union but in all countries.

AGGRESSION AND ITS DEFINITION

Having found its theoretical way to acknowledgment of a general law of nations, the Soviet Union assumed the leading role in a campaign to establish among its norms a definition of aggression. In Article 10 of the Covenant, the members of the League of Nations undertook "to respect and preserve as against external aggression the territorial integrity and existing political independence of all members." That was half a century ago, and one of the most agitated questions in the whole intervening period has been whether and how to define aggression. There has never ceased to be a respectable body of opinion that opposes the attempt at definition and would leave every case to contemporary appreciation in the light of its inevitably peculiar circumstances. Some have argued that a fixed definition would narrow the prohibition; while others, taking the opposite tack, have feared that it might be used to inculpate a state acting with serious reason from motives of pure self-defense. Constantly changing methods of using power, it is observed by both these schools, alter the forms of attack and the dimensions of self-defense. There remains, however, quite enough belief, especially on the part of the Soviet Union and its supporters, to keep the question on the international agenda in spite of massive and repeated fail-

[4] See also his *Droit international public* (Paris, 1965), p. 186.

ures to win general acceptance for any formula, whether cast in abstract terms or enumerating concrete acts.

This is one of the many international problems in which the essential difficulty is the absence of a general and supreme judicial authority. Given such authority, it would be enough to lay down the rule that any use or threat of force by one state against another, otherwise than in self-defense or in execution of a mandate from the organized world community, would constitute the international crime of aggression. Needless to say, neither the definition nor the judgment would do more than begin to solve the problem. Here, as elsewhere, the keeping or restoration of the peace presupposes an effective executive organ.

One of the earliest attempts at definition, in Article 10 of the abortive Geneva Protocol of 1924,[5] began by declaring an aggressor any state that resorted to war in violation of the Covenant of the League or of the Protocol. It added a presumption of aggression, rebuttable only by unanimous finding of the League Council, against any state engaging in hostilities in disregard of a unanimous recommendation or report of the Council, or after refusing to submit a dispute to pacific settlement or to comply with a judicial decision or arbitral award. To limit what might otherwise be an endless and evasive debate as to the interpretation of this Article, Article 20 imposed the obligation to submit to the Permanent Court of International Justice any dispute as to the meaning of the text. We have seen how what might have been a notable advance towards peace and security was defeated by second thoughts in Great Britain and the Dominions.

In 1933 the USSR provided a model that was adopted almost verbatim by the Security Committee of the Disarmament Conference. This set the form of a list of acts, any one of which would constitute aggression on the part of the

[5] Above, pp. 39-40.

states first resorting to it. The list included declaration of war; armed invasion; attack on territory, ships, or aircraft; naval blockade; assistance to invading armed bands. The same definition was inserted in the nonaggression treaties concluded in 1933 by the Soviet Union with eleven countries in Europe and the Middle East.

After the war the Soviet Union returned to the attack on aggression, when, in 1950, it proposed its formula of the 1930's for general adoption in the General Assembly of the United Nations. The General Assembly referred this draft to the International Law Commission, which, after eleven meetings, reported in favor of the abstract type of definition, observing that no list of aggressive acts could be exhaustive, and it must leave the ground open for new kinds of attack. The Commission was unable, however, to accept Dr. Alfaro's draft, which would have brought up to date and made somewhat more explicit the formula of Article 10 of the Geneva Protocol. The text, which follows, harmonizes perfectly with the principal purpose of the United Nations: "Aggression is the threat or use of force by a state or government against another state, in any manner, whatever the weapons employed and whether openly or otherwise, for any reason, or for any purpose other than individual or collective self-defense or in pursuance of a decision or recommendation by a competent organ of the United Nations." It could well be generally accepted but for the fact that important states take the view defended by Julius Stone in his *Aggression and World Order*, namely that it is still legal to use force where no collective organization provides reliable assurance of justice.

No less than thirty-five meetings of the Sixth (Legal) Committee of the General Assembly at the 1951 and 1952 sessions were devoted to the question, and since 1952 the General Assembly has had special committees, first of fifteen, then of nineteen, and finally of thirty-five jurists, inconclusively working upon it. Weeks of discussion in the

1968 and 1969 meetings of the Committee in Geneva and New York ended without an agreed definition. While asserting that progress had been made, the best that the Committee could do was to ask the General Assembly for more time.[6]

Unwilling to concede the necessity of subjection to a common judicial authority, but committed to the principle that something must be done to curb the evil of aggression, governments thus languidly persist in the vain search for a formula which is at once adequate and automatically applicable.

PEACEFUL COEXISTENCE

The alleged product of socialist legal development in which Communist writers take most pride is the group of slogans known now as the "Five Principles of Peaceful Co-existence." First announced in a communiqué published on July 1, 1954 after a meeting between Prime Ministers Nehru and Chou En-lai, and subsequently endorsed by the Bandung Conference of 1955, these took the following form in the Program of the Communist Party of the USSR:

1. Renunciation of war and substitution of pacific means of settling disputes

2. Equality, understanding, and trust among states, with full consideration of each other's interests

3. Nonintervention in internal affairs, and recognition of every people's right to decide all questions concerning itself

4. Strict respect for the sovereignty and territorial integrity of all states

5. Economic and cultural cooperation in full equality and for mutual advantage

[6] See UN Doc. A/AC134/5, April 7, 1969. On the whole subject of development and codification by the UN see Rosalyn Higgins, *The Development of International Law Through the Political Organs of the United Nations* (London, 1963).

57

To anyone acquainted with the proceedings of international agencies and the language of diplomatic conferences since 1920, these "Five Principles" are at least as familiar as the ten commandments. Their effective implementation would solve all the problems of world politics: their proclamation solves none. No one will begrudge the Communist claim to their invention if the policies of the proclaiming states begin to conform with them. The example might well prove as infectious as the violence that is their antithesis. In any event, they have been considered serious enough to warrant General Assembly instructions to its Sixth Committee to formulate "The International Law of Peaceful Relations." Literally this would mean the whole law of that world community which the Charter of the United Nations purported to inaugurate. The General Assembly, however, was content to direct the Committee to concentrate upon seven principles enshrined in the Charter with a view to achieving international consensus upon their implications. The principles specified were the following:

a) States shall refrain from the threat or use of force

b) States shall settle their disputes by peaceful means

c) States shall not intervene in matters within the domestic jurisdiction of other states

d) States shall cooperate with one another in accordance with the Charter

e) The principle of equal rights and self-determination of peoples

f) The sovereign equality of states

g) States shall fulfill in good faith the obligation of the Charter

With the exception of the injunction to fulfill obligations in good faith, these seven principles would appear to add nothing to the five enunciated in the Communist Program, unless perhaps that the prohibition of force is to be interpreted as broader than the renunciation of war and substitution of pacific settlement. In any event, the Soviet Union will probably find no greater difficulty in reconciling its support of "wars of liberation" with the seven than with its own five principles of peaceful coexistence.

The initial task of discovering and formulating the degree of international consensus upon the seven principles was assigned to a special committee of thirty-one members reporting through the Sixth Committee to the General Assembly. In its 1968 session the Assembly requested the Special Committee to endeavor to finish its work and submit a comprehensive report in 1969. This it was unable to do, and the Assembly asked it to reconvene in the first half of 1970 (Resolution 2533).

It would seem in any event that the "International Law of Peaceful Relations" was substantially covered by the agenda drawn up by the International Law Commission at its first meeting, in 1949. The list of subjects then selected for codification was as follows:

1. Recognition of states and governments
2. Succession of states and governments
3. Jurisdictional immunities of states and their property
4. Jurisdiction with regard to crimes committed outside national territory
5. Regime of the high seas
6. Regime of territorial waters
7. Nationality, including statelessness
8. Treatment of aliens
9. Right of asylum
10. Law of treaties
11. Diplomatic intercourse and immunities
12. Consular intercourse and immunities
13. State responsibility
14. Arbitral procedure

59

In its twenty years of operation, the Commission, meeting annually in a two-month session, has completed its work on six of these items, namely numbers 5, 6, 10, 11, 12, and 14. In addition, it prepared drafts for the conventions on the territorial shelf and high seas fisheries drawn up at Geneva in 1958, along with those on the regime of the high seas and territorial waters, and for the convention on statelessness concluded in 1961. At the special request of the General Assembly, it also formulated the principles of the Nuremberg Trials and drafted a declaration on the rights and duties of states and a code of offenses against the peace and security of mankind. All told, this is a remarkable achievement in view of the political antagonisms obstructing progress. The stubborn objection of the Soviet Union to articles in the draft on arbitration that would have made continuation of the procedure obligatory once it had been initiated reduced what set out to be a convention to the humbler status of model rules which governments may or may not follow. Work on the responsibility of states, one of the subjects that defeated the League's codification conference in 1930, is still in an indecisive stage, held up by the old disagreements about standards of justice, the effect of an alien's waiver of the right to ask for intervention by his government (the Calvo clause), and the obligation to compensate when alien property is taken over in a program of nationalization.

If the place of the recognition of states and governments as number 1 on its list had meant that the Commission believed no aspect of international relations to be more in need of agreed formulation than this, there would have been excellent reason for its priority in the agenda. It is under this rubric that international lawyers have traditionally placed the qualifications for and attainment of statehood and so of membership in that world community whose law was to be developed and codified. Surely nothing could be more fundamental to a world legal order in the making than the identification of its subjects; yet on this threshold question doctrine and practice alike have been confused, ambiguous, and contradictory. The Commission did not in fact put recognition first in its working timetable, choosing rather the formulation of the law of treaties, which may well have appeared less politically formidable, though it was to prove a long and arduous task.

Attempts have of course been made by writers to formulate a rational and coherent law of recognition or at least to point out the broad lines of regulation. Notable among them are those by Professor (now Judge) P. C. Jessup and by the late Professor and Judge Sir Hersch Lauterpacht. The latter's formulation, though distinguished by the idealism and the profound legal scholarship characteristic of its author, is marred by what seems to me the contradiction of asserting the constitutive effect of recognition and yet attributing to the unrecognized entity a legal right to be recognized.[7] Judge Jessup's study of the problem is of a highly practical nature and suggests effective means of dealing with it. What he recommends is a declaration by the General Assembly of the United Nations defining the attributes of statehood, making their possession a question to be decided exclusively by the General Assembly acting upon the recommendation of the Security Council, as now in the admission of new members, and prohibiting independent recognition by members of the United Nations. The United Nations would thus become the sole authority for the recognition of new states, a development that Professor Jessup thought desirable as making for the universality of that Organization, since recognition of statehood and admission to membership would result from one and the same collec-

[7] *Recognition in International Law* (Cambridge, 1943), pp. 73-78.

61

tive decision.[8] In what follows it will be seen that I reach similar, though not identical, conclusions.

According to the constitutive theory, statehood and participation in the international legal order are attained by political groups only insofar as they are recognized by established states. The declaratory doctrine is to the effect that once a political group has established itself in a defined territory under independent and apparently stable government and has given evidence of willingness and ability to comply with international obligations, it becomes a state member of the "family of nations." Recognition is merely acknowledgment of the fact that the status has been attained. Some adherents of this doctrine assert that the new state has a right to recognition, and one British government adopted this view,[9] though most states take the position that recognition is a political act depending entirely on the discretion of each government. The practice of states, then, is heavily against any right to recognition.[10] Yet it is now generally admitted that once a group has acquired the characteristics above-mentioned it must be treated in accordance with international law. To attack it without provocation and without declaration of war, or to treat its members without regard for the norms on the treatment of aliens in a state's territory, would be as much a violation of international law as if the territory or aliens concerned belonged to a recognized state. What, then, is left of recognition if it does not determine the right to be treated in accordance with the law? Little if anything more than this, that states retain the liberty to manifest their approval or disapproval by granting or refusing recognition. Formal and direct diplomatic relations will not be established be-

[8] A Modern Law of Nations (New York, 1948), pp. 43-51.

[9] Great Britain, Parliamentary Debates (Commons), vol. 485 (1950-51), pp. 2410-11.

[10] Cf. memo prepared by UN Secretariat, Security Council Official Records, 5th year (1950), special supp. no. 1, pp. 19-20.

fore recognition;[11] but this does not differentiate recognition from nonrecognition, since the establishment and continuance of diplomatic relations with recognized states is a matter of discretion, and the breaking off of diplomatic interchange does not signify withdrawal of recognition either of the state or of its government.

If it were clearly understood and generally acknowledged by governments that the only significance of recognition and nonrecognition is that the former indicates willingness to entertain normal relations while the latter suggests an intention to keep contacts to a minimum, it would be relatively simple to clear up the remaining confusions surrounding the subject. We should be spared the now frequent anomaly of an attitude commonly interpreted as refusal to admit the statehood and membership in the international legal community of an entity which is nevertheless admitted to have rights and duties under the law of that community. We should also be spared the absurdity of a state's sharing the rights and duties established by the Charter and yet maintaining that this does not constitute its recognition of a member as being either *de facto* or *de jure* a state person in the general legal order. This paradox, which is all the more striking since admission is limited to states,[12] exists only by virtue of the doctrine that recognition by individual states is a status-creating act. If nonrecognition merely expresses disapproval of the new member and the intention to have as little as possible to do with it, we may deplore this attitude while still considering it permissible.

We should still be left with the question: who determines whether or not a claimant group has the qualifications of statehood? As a first step toward solving this problem, we

[11] These may take the form of a single act. The establishment of diplomatic relations without previous formal declaration of recognition is held to imply recognition.

[12] Art. 4.

might try to obtain a clear and agreed definition of those qualifications, for instance along the lines followed by the League's Permanent Mandates Commission when it specified the conditions justifying independent statehood for territories under mandate.[13] Since any group satisfying such conditions will, judging now by twenty-three years of experience, almost certainly desire the prestige and other advantages of membership in the United Nations, its application could be treated at the same time as a submission of its claim to statehood, and its admission accepted as a conclusive certificate of this status and of international personality. This procedure may of course keep worthy applicants on the waiting list; but no mode of formal matriculation can exclude political preferences from the process of decision.

Kelsen, declaring himself forced to abandon the declaratory in favor of the constitutive theory, distinguishes between legal and political recognition. It is the former that is constitutive, and Kelsen does not shrink from the consequence that if the legal existence of a state depends upon recognition by states already established, a community may be a state in relation to some states and a nonstate in relation to others. This is for him a common and unavoidable characteristic of a "system" so decentralized that each subject determines for itself whether a fact to which international law attaches legal consequences exists or does not exist.[14] I have already argued that such a degree of decentralization negates the essential character of a legal system. The international order is a legal system in the making, its progress to be measured in terms of its centralization.

[13] League Doc. c, 442; M. 176, 1931. vi, vi A Mandates, 1931. viai, 229. For summary see G. H. Hackworth, *Digest of International Law* (Washington, D.C., 1940) 1: 119-20. All cited in Jessup, *op.cit.*, p. 45, n. 10.

[14] *Principles of International Law*, pp. 389-95.

My contention, then, is that individual recognition has no longer any legal significance save within the legal system of the recognizing state. Within certain limits, that system may, for internal purposes, attach different legal consequences to recognized and unrecognized communities. The simple fact is that all parties to the Charter have legally recognized the statehood of every community admitted to membership of the United Nations. Article 4 of the Charter lays it down that membership is open to "peace-loving states," and I take this to mean that only such entities may be admitted. If so, admission by "decision of the General Assembly upon the recommendation of the Security Council" is a certificate of statehood, and all states, in becoming parties to the Charter, give advance recognition as states to every community receiving this certification.

Individual acts of recognition may properly be described as "political" or "diplomatic." For reasons that seem good to them, governments may find it expedient to express their approval or disapproval of a new state by limiting their dealings with it to matters in which they perceive a clear national interest. In such cases, they are at liberty to withhold political or diplomatic recognition and may sustain this attitude by explicit provisos that no business transacted by them with the community in question is to be interpreted as recognition.

Any draft convention prepared by the International Law Commission to settle the law on this subject should, then, begin by laying down the firm principle that any community established in independent control of territory with a good prospect of permanency, and with the will and ability to fulfill the international obligations arising out of its history and present situation, is a state, and must be treated as such by other states irrespective of recognition or membership in the United Nations. The International Law Commission could here take a leaf from the Montevideo Convention of 1933, which asserts the existence of states before recognition.

The need for clarity on this point is demonstrated by the fact that admission to the United Nations may be blocked by veto in the Security Council, and a community that has achieved the attributes of statehood may be kept waiting for this certification and for unilateral recognitions. In such circumstances, of course, there is as yet nothing to prohibit governments from denying that the applicant community is qualified, and unless provision is made for compulsory reference of the question of fact to adjudication, this negative attitude may be indefinitely prolonged. For this reason, a convention laying down the principle will constitute little practical progress unless it stipulates submission of any dispute to an impartial body such as the International Court of Justice.

The recognition of governments is a different matter, but one clouded with similar ambiguities. What is involved is not the acknowledgment of statehood, but the decision as to who is entitled to act for a given state. Here again states claim unfettered discretion, and again nonrecognition may not signify doubt as to who actually governs but moral or moralistic disapproval and political antagonism. Material consequences may attend nonrecognition in this context, for national courts have often refused to admit the validity of acts done by unrecognized governments in cases where this negative decision has affected title to property or personal rights.[15] The political consequences are at once serious and ludicrous—serious because of stubborn impediments to grievously needed international cooperation; ludicrous be-

[15] See for example the series of cases in American courts summarized in Hackworth, *Digest*, 1: 364-87; and for Great Britain, Luther V. Sagor, 1 K.B., 456 and 3 K.B., 532. See also D. W. Greig, "The Carl Zeiss Case and The Position of an Unrecognized Government in English Law," LQR, January 1967, pp. 96ff.

cause of the flagrant unreason of the postures assumed and the antics adopted to get round the impediments. These distortions and their deplorable results are all vividly displayed in the dealings of the United States and a number of other countries with the Chinese People's Republic.

What is practically a government in exile on an island seventy miles off the Chinese mainland, viable only in virtue of American military, economic, and diplomatic support, and controlling with that support less than two percent of the Chinese population, is officially held by the majority of states to be the *de jure* government of China's immense territory and seven hundred million people. It is necessary at times, however, and at others merely profitable, to deal with the world's most populous nation, and on these occasions nonrecognizing governments, while carefully stipulating that what they are doing is not to be interpreted as recognition of Peking even as *de facto* government of China, negotiate and conclude agreements with its delegates. To avoid infection at home, a remote capital may be chosen for these meetings. Such is the pantomime we are forced to witness when the title to govern is left to the subjective appreciation of individual states.

Where a great nation is involved, there is obviously universal interest in an objective and authoritative decision of the question of who is entitled to govern and represent it. But the interest is also substantial in cases of less spectacular prominence. Again the decision should be in the hands of an organization representing that universality, and the United Nations is our nearest approach. Agreement that the committees which pass upon credentials of delegates to the General Assembly and the Security Council should by their decision confirm or deny, in such a way as to bind all members, the title of the delegates' senders to govern, would be a long step in the right direction.

The complex mechanism of the United Nations is our furthest advance toward a supranational legislature, and the International Law Commission has proved its merits not only as a standing drafting committee, but as a body where, in spite of the nonofficial character of its members, even the political and cultural differences of their countries undergo a first round of reconciliation. In this latter role, the Commission is ever more valuable since the doubling of United Nations membership. The enlargement of the Commission from the original fifteen experts in 1948 to twenty-five in 1961 gives new assurance that all main currents of legal thought will find representation, and at the same time gives the newly established nations of Asia and Africa a necessary sense of participation in the adaptation to present needs of a legal order which they had little or no part in elaborating.

Where the object is a convention, the draft worked out by the Commission and submitted to the General Assembly may be passed on to a diplomatic conference. There it is examined article by article and may be considerably altered. After adoption by what is now usually a two-thirds vote of the conference, it is open for ratification or accession and comes into force after a stated period following a specified number of such acceptances. Thus the great conventions drawn up at Geneva in 1958 on the law of the sea stipulated that they would come into force thirty days after the twenty-second ratification or adherence. No one acquainted with the involved and contentious procedure of national legislation should be surprised at the complexities and delays of this long-drawn-out process in a milieu where the differences to be compromised are aggravated by a multitude of factors not present, or present in much weaker form, in the national arena.

So the time may be long before the codifying conventions of the United Nations have won sufficient official acceptance to establish them indisputably as world law. They are, however, by no means without value meanwhile, for they embody a broad juristic consensus that will inevitably be reflected in judicial and arbitral decisions and in learned treatises. Precedent and doctrine will thus spread their acceptance independently of formal ratification.

Authority of the same kind and of at least equal weight attaches to General Assembly Resolutions declaring principles of law, especially when these are unanimous, as were those of 1961 and 1963 on space. These proclaimed the principles that space should never be used for other than peaceful purposes, that no nuclear weapons or other weapons of mass destruction should be put in orbit, stationed in outer space or installed on celestial bodies, that celestial bodies should not be subject to national appropriation, and that international law extended to human activities in space. They went on to record agreement that the launching state is responsible for all damages caused to aliens by their spacecraft and that such craft and their personnel, landing in foreign territory, should be returned to the launching country.

All these principles were incorporated in the Treaty on Principles Governing the Activities of States in the Exploration and Use of Outer Space including the Moon and Other Celestial Bodies, signed at Washington, London, and Moscow on January 27, 1967. This came into force on October 10, 1967 in accordance with Article XIV, 3, when ratification had been deposited by five governments, including those of the United States, the United Kingdom, and the Soviet Union, which are designated in the Treaty as Depositary Governments. By March 1, 1967, no less than sixty-two states, not including France or the Chinese People's Republic, had signed the instrument. This is one of the instances where norms prepounded by the General Assembly have later been cast in the most imperative form available in the world community.

69

LAW OF THE SEA

We must now examine in some detail the progress toward codification made under the auspices of the United Nations or otherwise since 1945. In spite of its failure to reach agreement upon the width of the territorial sea, the Geneva Conference of 1958, carrying on the invaluable work of the International Law Commission, made a noteworthy advance toward a definitive code for coastal waters as well as for the continental shelf and the high sea. This important sector of international relations has been marked by uncertainty and controversy that has reduced the scope of consensus to principles so abstract as to permit intolerable divergencies of practice. The four conventions adopted by the Conference, so far as they are ratified, will define and register consensus upon many points hitherto in dispute. Insofar as ratifying states also subscribe to the Optional Protocol for the Compulsory Settlement of Disputes, the result will be a statutory and judicial regime that will lack only reliable provision for enforcement. In the respect last mentioned, parties can of course invoke Article 94 of the United Nations Charter if they have a judgment of the International Court of Justice in their favor; but this, as already noted, may for political reasons prove a weak reed.[16]

Clearly, the absence of an agreed limit to the marginal belt of sea in which a riparian state has full sovereignty, subject to the right of innocent passage, leaves room for dangerous disputes. That this was fully realized is shown by the decision to hold a second conference on this question and the allied one of exclusive fishing rights. That conference, convened at Geneva in 1960, also failed to settle these points. Meanwhile, however, there have been increasing manifestations of usage contrary to the position held by the United States as the most obstinate champion of the

[16] Above, p. 28.

three-mile rule. Bilateral and multilateral negotiations, and a number of unilateral declarations, indicate a growing tendency to assert, or to acquiesce in, state sovereignty over a marginal belt of twelve miles.[17] The 1958 Convention itself set a boundary of twelve miles, measured from the base line for territorial waters, to the contiguous zone in which the state may exercise control for customs, fiscal, immigration, or sanitary purposes (Art. 24). Though the Article is in permissive rather than restrictive form, international courts may well take it as setting an outer maritime frontier beyond which no legal claim to territorial sovereignty may extend. On the principle that states may do anything not prohibited by international law, judgment would even now probably go against defenders of any lesser limit. Even if a court might find an adequate past consensus supporting the three-mile rule, proof of a present majority against that limit would justify an opinion that international law does not now prohibit treating the whole twelve-mile zone as territorial. Until a definite limit has been agreed upon by the great maritime powers, however, these will be loath to submit disputes on the question to adjudication or other form of pacific settlement. It is not surprising that France, the Soviet Union, the United Kingdom, and the United States have all failed (December 31, 1967) to ratify the Optional Protocol providing for the compulsory settlement of disputes arising out of the Law of the Sea Convention.[18]

What, then, are the positive contributions of the 1958 Conventions to the law of the sea? To attempt anything approaching a complete answer would be to add another to the lengthy treatises already elicited by this question.[19]

[17] Below, p. 73.

[18] See *Multilateral Treaties, 1968*.

[19] For detailed analysis, the reader is referred to such works as Myres S. McDougal and William T. Burke, *The Public Order of the Oceans* (New Haven, 1962); C. John Colombos, *The International Law of the Sea*, 6th rev. ed. (London, 1967).

Only selected points, indicating the nature and importance of a great legislative effort, can be touched upon here. These are: (*a*) in the Convention on the Territorial Sea: base lines, bays, innocent passage, public ships; (*b*) in the Convention on the High Seas: rights of landlocked states, nationality of ships and jurisdiction over them, piracy and pollution; (*c*) in the Convention on Fisheries and Conservation of Living Resources: conservation areas, special interests of coastal states, and the handling of disputes; (*d*) in the Convention on the Continental Shelf: measurement, and restrictions on the rights of coastal states.

The Territorial Sea

BASE LINES. As "normal base line for measuring the breadth of the territorial sea," Article 3 of this Convention re-affirms the traditional low-water mark. The important development here is the acceptance of straight base lines under the conditions sketched by the International Court of Justice in the *Anglo-Norwegian Fisheries* case in 1951, together with the formulation of new norms to prevent the drawing of these lines in such a way as to depart appreciably from the general direction of the coast, to safeguard existing liberties of innocent passage, and to preserve the rights of neighboring coastal states.

BAYS. One of the unsettled questions in the law of the sea has been that of national sovereignty in bays. Many states claim sovereignty by right of long control in "historic bays" that in some cases exceed thirty miles at the mouth, and there has been a reciprocating acquiescence in such claims. But for bays in general international law lacked both an established definition and a rule to determine where territorial waters ended and the high sea began.

Following an example set by the Franco-British Convention of August 2, 1839 and the North Seas Fisheries Convention of May 6, 1882, the tribunal in the North Atlantic Fisheries Arbitration of 1910 recommended a norm that classified bays not more than ten miles wide at the mouth as internal waters of the riparian state. Where the mouth was wider, the line was to be drawn at the point nearest the mouth where the breadth narrowed to ten miles. Three miles of water outside this line was classed as territorial.[20] In harmony with broadening claims to territorial waters, Article 7 of the 1958 Territorial Sea Convention adopts a twenty-four mile line. The Convention also provides a mathematical formula to distinguish bays from other coastal indentations.

INNOCENT PASSAGE AND PUBLIC VESSELS. We shall later be concerned with the indeterminably subjective elements in most of the definitions formulated in the four conventions. Innocent passage affords a good example. Passage is said (Art. 14.4) to be innocent "so long as it is not prejudicial to the peace, good order or security of the coastal state." Of the four key words here, "prejudicial," "peace," "good order," and "security," each is susceptible to a wide variety of interpretation, and states will cling stubbornly to their own meanings.

The same vagueness attaches to the stated condition under which a state may temporarily suspend innocent passage, namely that "suspension is essential for its security." On the other hand, there is no lack of clarity in such norms as that "Submarines are required to navigate on the surface and to show their flag" (Art. 14.6); that "There shall be no suspension of innocent passage for foreign ships through straits which are used for international navigation between one part of the high seas and another part of the high seas or the territorial sea of a foreign state" (Art. 16.4); or that

[20] On the whole subject see S. Whittemore Boggs, "Delimitation of Seaward Areas under National Jurisdiction," AJIL, 45 (1951), 240-66.

the rules applicable to merchant ships "shall also apply to government ships operated for commercial purposes" (Art. 21). The first of these three norms was designed to meet a substantial objection of the United States to the extension of the territorial sea, namely that submarines could take refuge from belligerent attack in the deeper offshore waters of neutral states. The second norm would prevent closure of such passages as the Corfu Straits, or the Straits of Tiran leading from the Red Sea to territorial waters of Saudi Arabia, the United Arab Republic, and Israel, in the Gulf of Aqaba.[21] The third may terminate a long-standing difference in the treatment accorded to public trading vessels by the United States and Great Britain on the one hand and by an increasing number of countries on the other. In other words, the Convention may herald the end of the immunities hitherto granted by these two great maritime powers. ("May," because presumably they will not be prohibited from granting such immunities if they decide to continue doing so.)

The High Seas

LANDLOCKED STATES. Article 3 of the Convention on the High Seas is a striking manifestation of community interest in improving the position of members seriously handicapped by circumstances beyond their control. It reads: "States situated between the sea and a state having no seacoast shall by common agreement with the latter and in conformity with existing international conventions accord . . . free transit through their territory . . . and to ships fly-

[21] Charles B. Selak, Jr., "A Consideration of the Legal Status of the Gulf of Aqaba," AJIL, 52 (1958), 660; "The Aqaba Question in International Law," *Egyptian Review of International Law*, 13 (1957), 86; Hamad, "The Right of Passage in the Gulf of Aqaba," *ibid.*, 15 (1959), 118; all cited by W. W. Bishop, *International Law: Cases and Materials* (Boston, 1962), 2nd ed., p. 499, n. 84.

ing the flag of that state treatment equal to that accorded to their own ships, or to the ships of any other state, as regards access to seaports and the use of such ports." The interest served is not solely the promotion of international trade; humanitarian considerations played a part here as they do in international aid in the modernization of underdeveloped countries.

The language, it will be noted, is imperative. The imperative is repeated in Article 3.2, where it is laid down that "all matters relating to freedom of transit and equal treatment in ports" shall be settled by mutual agreement. Strictly, of course, these are nothing more than commands to negotiate, since it is not possible to oblige any one to agree. This fact makes the outcome all the more noteworthy. The Convention on Transit Trade of Landlocked States drawn up at New York in 1965 was signed within that year by no less than twenty-nine states, and came into force on June 9, 1967, on ratification by two land-locked and two transit states. By September 1968, there were fifteen acceptances by ratification or accession.

NATIONALITY OF SHIPS. Article 5 leaves to each state the determination of the conditions under which its nationality can be acquired by ships, just as general international law leaves it to each state to decide who are its nationals. The text, however, adds the proviso that there must be "a genuine link" between the state and the ship. This was suggested by the judgment in the *Nottebohm* case, where the International Court of Justice held that the right of diplomatic protection in behalf of a naturalized citizen depended upon a substantial relationship between that national and the naturalizing state. ("Conferred by a state, it [nationality] only entitles that state to exercise protection vis-à-vis another state, if it constitutes a translation into

75

juridical terms of the individual's connection with the state which has made him its national.")[22] Whereas, however, the Court specified certain criteria of an adequate relationship, such as "a social fact of attachment, a genuine connection of existence, interests and sentiments, together with the existence of reciprocal rights and duties," the only guide offered by the Convention is that "in particular, the state must effectively exercise its jurisdiction and control in administrative, technical and social matters over ships flying its flag." Does this include the general policing of the ship on the high seas and elsewhere, together with responsibility for the consequences of any failure to measure up to international standards? If so, it may check the issue of "flags of convenience" by states ill equipped for such supervision.[23] In any event, this Article, in harmony with the rest of the Convention, emphasizes the growing tendency in international deliberations to treat the oceans as public domain of a world community in which freedom of use should be subject to law enacted and enforced in that community's behalf.

JURISDICTION OF FLAG STATE. In the *Lotus* case, the Permanent Court of International Justice held that "there is no rule of international law in regard to collision cases to the effect that criminal proceedings are exclusively within the jurisdiction of the state whose flag is flown."[24] Much of the strongly supported dissenting opinion was based on the view that the state of the flag had exclusive jurisdiction. Insofar as it is adopted, Article 11 of the Convention on the High Seas will establish the rule that the Court could not find in its extensive researches. Exclusive jurisdiction is given to the flag state, save when the accused person is a

[22] ICJ *Reports*, 1955, p. 23.
[23] See McDougal and Burke, *op.cit.*, pp. 1013, 1015, 1025, 1033-34.
[24] PCIJ, 1927, series A, no. 10.

national of another state, which then has concurrent jurisdiction. The Article concludes with the decisive provision that "No arrest or detention of the ship, even as a measure of investigation, shall be ordered by any authorities other than those of the flag state." Everything that a verbal formula can do has thus been done to terminate an acute disagreement.

PIRACY. Article 15 would put an end to the contention that states may treat as pirates *jure gentium* persons who engage in violence on the high seas in furtherance of a rebellion that has not yet attained the status of insurgency. Where the political motive is clear and dominant, no act, however classified and however punishable under municipal law, would satisfy the Convention's definition of piracy. Useful, too, is the inclusion of acts of violence by the crew or passengers of aircraft or against aircraft on the high seas or in any other place outside the jurisdiction of any state, and of similar acts by a public ship or aircraft whose crew has mutinied and taken control.

POLLUTION. Again the conception of the high seas as public domain, *res publica* rather than the *res communis* of earlier doctrine, is prominent in the new norms of Articles 24 and 25, which require states to take measures to prevent pollution by oil or radioactive waste.

Fishing and Conservation

President Truman's two proclamations of September 28, 1945, the first announcing the United States Government's intention to establish conservation zones in contiguous areas of the high seas where fishing had been or might be carried on on a substantial scale, the second declaring the right of jurisdiction and control in the exploitation of the natural resources of the continental shelf, touched off a

77

train of national declarations of a similar or more drastic tenor. Full advantage was taken of the absence in the Truman proclamations of any definition of contiguity or continental shelf, and some of the South American claims extended as much as two hundred miles from shore. A number of states took the occasion to assert sovereignty not only over the shelf but in the waters covering it. The United States protested these arbitrary extensions of its initiative; while Great Britain went so far as to deny any national right to control fishing beyond the territorial sea, a position opposing even the relatively modest claims of the United States.[25] Memories of the Declaration of Panama, 1939, were still fresh. In this the Foreign Ministers of the American Republics had purported to establish a "security zone" extending three hundred miles seaward and surrounding the Western Hemisphere from its southern tip to the boundary of the United States and Canada. The time was ripe for a major collective effort to set limits to a movement that threatened appropriation or control of vast areas of the high seas.

CONSERVATION ZONES. The International Law Commission of the United Nations drafted the long series of articles that provided the basis of discussion and most of the text for the Geneva Conference of 1958 on the Law of the Sea. The Convention on Fishing and Conservation of the Living Resources of the High Seas (Art. 6 and 7) recognizes the special interest of a coastal state "in the maintenance of the productivity of the living resources in any area of the high seas adjacent to its territorial sea," and permits it to take unilateral action of the kind proclaimed by President Tru-

[25] For us protests to Chile, Peru, and Argentina, and the British note to Ecuador, September 14, 1951, see M. W. Mouton, *The Continental Shelf* (The Hague, 1952), pp. 89-94, and ADI Rec. 1954, 1: 428-30.

man in such areas, provided that negotiations with other states concerned have not led to an agreement within six months. Measures taken under this condition are moreover valid against other states only if urgently needed for conservation, based upon scientific findings, and not discriminatory against foreign fishermen. Disputes about them must, at the request of any of the parties, be submitted to the special commission of five members provided for in Article 9, unless the parties agree to another method of peaceful settlement. The salutary obligation of reference to impartial decision is thus in this instance embodied in the Convention itself. In the other three Conventions it depends upon acceptance of the Optional Protocol.

When nationals of two or more states fish the same stocks in any area of the high seas, these states are bound, on the request of any one of them, to negotiate necessary conservation measures. If such measures, which, it should be noted, are not limited to areas adjacent to territorial waters, are notified to the Director-General of FAO, other states are bound, not later than seven months after such notification, to apply them to their own nationals (Art. 4 and 5). If they fail to do so, proceedings may be taken under Article 9. FAO thus becomes a repository of such measures and must notify them to any state specified by the initiating state or asking to be informed. The machinery for administering the regime in behalf of a world community is in the making.

The Continental Shelf

The claim of coastal states to sovereignty in the continental shelf, or at least to "jurisdiction and control" over its resources, is a development of the last four decades.[26] Usage was in process of growth that set the boundary to this dominion over "submerged land which is contiguous to the continent" at a point where the depth of water first

[26] See Mouton, *The Continental Shelf*, pp. 1-3, 6-12.

exceeded one hundred fathoms.[27] The 1958 Convention on the Continental Shelf stretches this "first" slightly by substituting 200 meters, and then indefinitely by an elastic extension "to where the depth of the superjacent waters admits of the exploitation of the natural resources of the said areas." So, the boundary advances seaward with improvements in the machinery of exploitation.

It is to be noted that Article 2 recognizes not sovereignty in the shelf, but only "sovereign rights for the purpose of exploring it and exploiting its natural resources." Thus the coastal state may not prevent "the laying or maintenance of submarine cables or pipe lines" on the seabed of the shelf as it may within the territorial sea; nor may it carry its exploration and exploitation to the point of "unjustifiable interference with navigation, fishing or conservation of the living resources of the sea," or of "any interference with fundamental oceanographic or other scientific research carried out with the intention of open publication." These Articles (4 and 5) are replete with debatable criteria such as "reasonable measures," "fundamental research," and "unjustifiable interference," and it is regrettable that we have not in this Convention any provision for compulsory settlement of disputes, but are dependent upon the Optional Protocol.

Happily the Convention sustains the position, announced in the Truman Proclamation of 1945, that the rights of the coastal state in the continental shelf have no effect "upon the legal status of the superjacent waters as high seas, or that of the air space above those waters."

DIPLOMATIC AND CONSULAR RELATIONS

The Convention adopted at the Conference on Diplomatic Relations held in Vienna in 1961 was, like those of Geneva on the law of the sea, the result of long preparatory work

[27] DSB, September 30, 1945, p. 484.

by the International Law Commission, and marks another step in the development and codification of international law under the auspices of the United Nations. It introduces a new classification of the heads and staffs of diplomatic missions and stipulates uniformity of practice in a number of matters, ranging from relatively important to trivial, in which there has hitherto been no common pattern.

The four classes of heads of mission adopted at Aix-la-Chapelle in 1818 are reduced to three by Article 14, the second category—envoys extraordinary and ministers plenipotentiary—being abandoned. Article 1 provides for the first time a classification of the entire personnel from head of mission to cook. This also is threefold—diplomatic, administrative and technical, and service staff—and the hierarchy is matched with appropriate gradations of privilege. Even the private domestics of members of a diplomatic mission are exempted from tax on their wages, though any further immunity depends upon the law of the receiving state.

Hitherto, Great Britain and the United States have held to the position that diplomatic agents do not lose their immunities when they engage in professional or commercial activities outside their official functions. Article 31 stipulates forfeiture of privilege in such circumstances, while Article 42 goes so far as to prohibit any profession or commercial activity for personal profit.

Article 32 settles a controversial question when it requires a distinct waiver for execution of judgment. No tacit or explicit acceptance of jurisdiction up to judgment is to be taken as covering execution.

The Convention does not recognize any duty on the part of third states to grant safe conduct to diplomatic agents on their way to or from their posts. If, however, a third state does allow passage to a diplomatic agent, as it normally does, it must accord him and his family "inviolability and such other immunities as may be required" for transit

81

(Art. 40). Here again, explicit norms replace doubt and diversity.

In 1963 a second conference at Vienna codified rules for consular relations. The result is a more liberal regime, bringing consular immunities and privileges closer to the diplomatic level. The Convention (Art. 31) generalizes the inviolability of consular premises, previously dependent upon special treaty. Except in cases of grave crime, Article 41 stipulates immunity from arrest or detention pending trial. Increased exemptions from taxes and customs duties are provided for in Articles 49 and 50, while Article 54 establishes immunities in third countries corresponding to those of diplomatic agents under the Convention of 1961. Like diplomatic agents, career consular officers are now prohibited from engaging in professional or commercial activities for personal profit (Art. 57).

The historical connection of the consular service with the protection of merchants and their interests has been an active factor in keeping it at a lower level of prestige. Ambassadors enjoyed the aristocratic glamor that gilds great affairs of state. In the last half-century the activities of the two forms of representation abroad have intermingled, and the tendency is to assimilate them in one foreign service. The assimilation of privileges is a natural accompaniment of the change, for insofar as this setting apart from the common lot is of any importance in the promotion of human welfare, it is hardly less important for one branch than for the other.

THE ANTARCTIC TREATY, 1959

We have seen how the multiplication of expanding national claims to control in ocean areas led to the international legislative conference at Geneva in 1958 and to the elaboration of a code that goes far to implement the conception of the seas as public domain of the human community. A simultaneous development, spurred on by worldwide scientific organizations planning multilateral cooperation in the International Geophysical Year (1957-1958), culminated in the Antarctic Treaty of 1959. This instrument, while explicitly avoiding any prejudice to the numerous overlapping claims to national sovereignty in the area, stipulates that "Antarctica shall be used for peaceful purposes only," a clause that we shall find repeated in various international declarations on space. The continent is therefore laid open in its entire extent to aerial inspection and to on-the-spot observation by persons appointed by any of the parties. Arrangements are made for the exchange of scientific personnel and data. Military activities and installations are prohibited, as are nuclear explosions and the testing of weapons. The twelve parties include all states that have asserted serious interests in the area,[28] and they have agreed that "no new claim or enlargement of an existing claim to territorial sovereignty in Antarctica shall be asserted while the present treaty is in force." Thus, without any explicit surrender of titles, the area takes on much of the character of world public domain. In view of the harmonious and fruitful collaboration that has prevailed under the treaty, which came into force in 1961, it is difficult to imagine that Antarctica will ever be divided into national compartments.

The Law of Treaties, 1969

The most elaborate single draft convention yet produced by the United Nations is that on the law of treaties finally adopted at Vienna in 1969. The ILC began work on this in 1949. One draft after another, prepared by a succession of distinguished *rapporteurs*, was put through the Commis-

---

[28] Argentina, Australia, Belgium, Chile, France, Japan, New Zealand, Norway, Republic of South Africa, USSR, USA, UK. For a brief summary of competing claims prior to 1959, see Corbett, *Law and Society in the Relations of States*, pp. 115-19.

sion's analytical screen at meeting after meeting, until the Preparatory Conference of 1968 initiated the stage of intergovernmental formulation. A second conference in the following year completed the 85-article text now submitted to states for final acceptance by ratification or accession. Treaties being now the chief mode of developing the law of nations, it was fitting that the utmost in the way of expert craftsmanship and responsible deliberation should be devoted to the codification of norms regulating their conclusion, interpretation, effects, and termination.

The Convention is a major attempt to end the many uncertainties in the customary law of treaties. It will doubtless elicit entire books of exegesis. Here a few examples suggesting the nature and scope of the enterprise must suffice.

Does the signature of a treaty text impose any obligation pending ratification? Yes; the signatory must "refrain from acts which would defeat the object and purpose of a treaty" (Art. 18). Can reservations be valid without the consent of all parties, and, if valid, what bearing have they upon the obligations of an objecting party? Here the Convention follows the Advisory Opinion of the International Court of Justice in regard to the Genocide Convention, adding elaborate detail to the conditions of validity and the bearing of reservations on parties other than the reserving state (Arts. 19-23). Is a state bound by a treaty to which its consent has been signified without the authority required by its internal law? Yes, unless the violation of that law "was manifest and concerned a rule . . . of fundamental importance" (Art. 46). These are all would-be final answers to questions long debated in doctrine and in diplomacy. At least equally important are the lengthy Articles (60-62) defining the conditions under which the breach of a treaty, supervening impossibility of performance or radical change of circumstances, may justify suspension or termination.

Probably nothing further in the way of verbal precision

could have been done for this central part of the law of nations. But the Convention abounds in qualifications that states will interpret with unrestrained subjectivity to accommodate their particular interests. For the settlement of disputes about interpretation and application, the parties will be committed to the obligations established by Chapter VI of the United Nations Charter; but experience has shown how indecisive these may be. The sole reference to the International Court of Justice occurs in Article 66, and this is limited to disputes arising under Articles 53 and 64 (peremptory norms—*jus cogens*). Failing agreement to arbitrate, any party to such a dispute may submit it to the ICJ "for decision." But is the other side bound by the decision? Once again we confront the weakness of verbal formulas not subject to compulsory and final interpretation by a standing tribunal independent of the parties in dispute.

Though they do not yet constitute world law, the great conventions elaborated since 1947 are monuments of expert work that has not only formulated rules and principles for new problems but significantly reduced the uncertainty of some important sectors of the existing international order. But no convention, however skillfully drafted, can eliminate the possibility of sharply opposing interpretations in its application to specific situations. Enactment is only part of the lawmaking process. Courts with the authority of binding interpretation complete it. The complete subjectivity of interpretation which reigns in the absence of compulsory jurisdiction draws out of law the regularity and predictability which are its purpose.

Two devices have been employed since the foundation of the League of Nations in an attempt to remedy this defect in the international legal order. One is the optional clause of Article 36.2 in the statute of the Permanent Court of International Justice and its successor the International Court of Justice by which states may accept in advance the Court's jurisdiction; the other is the now unhappily diminishing practice of inserting in conventions an article by which the parties undertake to submit to international adjudication disputes regarding the interpretation or application of the text. The first has had a disappointing history. Out of one hundred and twenty-six members of the United Nations in 1969, only forty-five had made declarations of acceptance under Article 36.2,[29] and many of these were weakened by reservations. The second device was adopted in a large number of conventions and for a time encouraged the hope that the developing treaty law of nations would be impartially interpreted. But this salutary practice has suffered a check. The Soviet Union, though a party to the Constitution of the International Labor Organization and to the Revised Slavery Convention of 1956, both of which contain the relevant article,[30] has in most cases displayed a marked unwillingness to be bound by any arrangement for interpretation. This negative attitude is in harmony with the Soviet thesis that impartial adjudication between socialist and capitalist states is virtually impossible, and goes far to explain the fact that the best that can now be done in conventions that aim at universality is to append a protocol in which parties may undertake to submit disputes about the text to impartial decision. States failing to do this retain all their traditional liberty of interpretation.[31]

Because the acceptance of jurisdiction is optional, the disputes actually submitted to the Court have not turned upon issues of the first importance. When such issues are involved, governments prefer to rely upon diplomatic maneuvering or their armed strength rather than impartial

[29] *Multilateral Treaties*, December 31, 1969.

[30] See above, p. 27.

[31] Cf. P. E. Corbett, *Law and Society in the Relations of States* (New York, 1951), pp. 13-14.

adjudication. As plausible justification for this preference they still plead the gaps and uncertainties in international law,[32] though the reduction of these defects by the case law and the lawmaking conventions of the last sixty years has not visibly increased their willingness to accept judicial or arbitral settlement. The real cause of the still strong opposition to compulsory jurisdiction lies much deeper; it has its roots in the narrowly conceived self-interest, built-in arrogance, and mutual distrust of sovereign states. If it were not so, the sober wisdom, high juristic competence, and profound appreciation of social values displayed by the bench of the World Court since its inauguration in 1922 would have done more than it has to change the negative official attitude.

The measure of the Court's contribution to the clarification and further elaboration of international law is not to be found in the material or political importance of the issues submitted to it. Appreciation of this fact by the judges explains the patient care and exhaustive research with which they have analyzed and weighed what must sometimes have seemed the trifling claims of the parties. Keeping strictly within the precise limits of the legal questions submitted, they have not failed to find in the existing body of norms the basis for judgments and opinions which, outside the Communist countries, have commanded unique respect.[33]

With all its cautious conservatism, the Court has enunciated principles never previously formulated, and won acceptance for them. It has in this way added to the content of international law. One notable example has already been

[32] The Advisory Committee of Jurists which in 1920 drafted the Statute of the PCIJ considered this plea serious enough to call for a program of codification under League auspices. See Records of the First Assembly, Plenary Meetings, p. 764.

[33] An exception to this generalization must be recognized in regard to the judgment of July 18, 1966 in the South West Africa cases.

discussed.[34] Another is the base line rule adopted in the Fisheries Case between the United Kingdom and Norway and in 1958 incorporated in the Geneva Convention on Territorial Waters. Norway asserted the right to prohibit foreign fishing in four miles of coastal waters measured from a base line parallel to the general direction of the fringe of islands along her coast. Great Britain, without disputing Norway's traditional claim to four miles of territorial waters, argued that the customary rule of international law placed the base line at low-water mark along the indentations of the coast. This would permit British fishing in some waters regarded by Norway as territorial. The Court held that the customary rule did not exclude straight base lines along a much-indented coast such as that of Norway. Its decision, recognizing the legality of an exception to the general rule, was influenced, if not determined, by the notoriety of Norway's practice and the long tolerance of it manifested by interested states, including Great Britain. Wide acceptance of the principle is indicated by its adoption in the Geneva Convention of 1958 and by the mathematical criteria established there for its application.

[34] See above, pp. 24-25.

4.

PROGRESS IN WORLD ORGANIZATION

FOR purposes of combat, the state is an ideal organization. Power and myth made it a formidable instrument, whether wielded by divine-right monarch or by popularly elected government.[1] Never merely the device by which a dominant class controlled and exploited its inferiors, as Marxist dogma would have it, the state could count upon a spontaneous tendency to patriotism. There was always the in-group feeling, the contempt, suspicion, or fear of the stranger, the sense of security and superiority derived from belonging. The humblest had privileges not granted to aliens. Nor was social mobility ever quite absent. The freedman might rise to high office. And, if the state offered honor, wealth, and a wide field of action to the strong, it offered the weak the illusion of identification with greatness, the pride of vicarious power.

So, to defend what the state already had, or to expand its possessions and glory at the expense of a neighbor, even a despotic government could mobilize voluntary and dedi-

[1] The central problem confronting the organization of world community has never been more strikingly put than by the scholar-statesman Karl Renner, between 1919 and 1950 successively Chancellor, Premier, Foreign Minister, and President of Austria. That problem is the effective submission of the modern state—with its claim to power unlimited by any law higher than its own over the property, life, and honor of those under its jurisdiction—to a degree of operative supranational authority adequate to the maintenance of peace and the orderly promotion of human welfare. See his *Mensch und Gesellschaft* (Vienna, 1952), p. 32 and *passim*.

cated service. If internal opposition threatened, it could be overcome by exaggerating or creating external dangers. Capitalist or Communist "encirclement" is a recent and familiar bogy. Legends of hereditary enmities maintained a tension that found exuberant release in war. Alliances to keep a balance of power were ephemeral expedients where waxing strength made the ally of today the menace of tomorrow.

Today's welfare state has added new claims to the life-and-death devotion of its citizens. The early political community furnished collective defense against marauding neighbors and organized raids in turn. In the Mediterranean cradle of civilization it managed irrigation, stored food, and systematized the propitiation of the gods. Hit-and-miss arrangements grew up for the settlement of disputes and for the punishment of acts deemed harmful to the community. The rest was left to family and clan. Out of these beginnings slowly grew elaborate military and legal systems. Some attention continued to be given to the stimulation of economic enterprise; but the prevailing conception of the function of government came to be one of maintaining a general setting within which approved private undertakings could flourish. It was only after the nineteenth-century industrial revolution that this doctrine came under serious and sustained attack. The attack has proceeded from victory to victory until now the state directs in intimate detail the conduct of each national and is fast assuming responsibility for his well-being from the cradle to the grave. The substitution of socialization for *laissez faire* is a global phenomenon; the state absorbs more and more of its population in official service, and its government concentrates about itself the human and material resources for the execution of duties which a century ago were thought to lie entirely outside of its proper role.

The nearest thing to universal orthodoxy in contemporary political philosophy is the doctrine that the state's reason for existence is the progressive improvement of the living conditions of those human beings over whom it has jurisdiction. Marxist dogma, indeed, clings to the myth that as Communism is attained, the state will "wither away," leaving its citizens in a condition of perfect cooperation eliminating all need for coercion. But while the masters of that ideology continue to preach that the state, invented to keep the toilers subservient to a master class, will have no place in a classless society, they append a warning that leaves the credo meaningless. If men, they say, are to achieve the high virtue and capacity necessary to the crime-less and stateless Communist life, they must first be purged of those survivals of capitalism that still give priority to selfish personal interest. If this fundamental obstacle to utopia is to be removed, the authority and power of the state must be raised to an historic peak. No other way leads to that apogee of human welfare which, they insist, only Communist society can reach. So long as the state exists, then, its purpose must be substantially the same as in the Western democracies. And if any Communist leader truly believes that the state is on its way out, none reveals in his policy any expectation that the way is to be short.

Communist or capitalist, surely the state described by President Renner has reached its apogee of power. Yet, however great the territory and power of the political com-munity, the demands of security and welfare alike reveal the inadequacies of organization that is cut off at national boundaries. It was already becoming obvious in nineteenth-century Europe that bilateral treaties of alliance or of friendship and commerce did not adequately meet the need of sustained international cooperation. Not mere agree-ments, but standing international organization, began to at-tract official attention as possible means.

The need of organized authority to keep order and im-

91

prove living conditions in a community of Europe had long been the subject of literary peace projects, some of them endorsed by ruling monarchs. For a brief period after the destructive upheaval of the French Revolution and the Napoleonic wars, similar dreams illumined official policy. In a type of reaction that was to be twice repeated in the first half of the twentieth century, the victorious Powers agreed in Article 6 of the treaty of November 20, 1815 "to renew at fixed intervals . . . meetings consecrated to great common objects and to the examination of such measures as at each of these epochs shall be judged most salutary for the peace and prosperity of the nations and for the maintenance of the peace of Europe." To the Concert of Europe thus inaugurated by Austria, Great Britain, Prussia, and Russia, the France of the restored Bourbons was admitted in 1818, and until 1822 this Great-Power directorate attempted to implement and complete the settlement reached at Vienna.

As an essay in international government, the series of congresses between 1815 and 1822 shows some interesting points of comparison with those inaugurated in 1920 and 1946. The results achieved at Aix-la-Chapelle in the Autumn of 1818 were positive enough to encourage high hopes. True, the "universal union of guarantee" proposed by Alexander I was firmly and effectively opposed by Great Britain in a rejection of broad continental commitments that was to be conspicuously repeated in 1919; but the Quadruple Alliance of 1815 was renewed and a declaration added to the effect that the Powers would maintain their close union, "strengthened by the ties of Christian brotherhood," to keep a peace based upon respect for treaties. The evacuation of France was unanimously agreed upon, and several questions of dynastic title and succession expeditiously settled. Time was even found to dispose of some long-vexed matters of diplomatic rank and precedence in a regulation that endured until 1961, when the flamboy-antly styled "Second Congress of Vienna" drafted a new one. Offsetting these successes, however, there were al-ready signs of the oppositions and distrusts that were soon to break up the "Grand Alliance." Among the decisions taken at the Congress of Vienna but still awaiting imple-mentation were those calling for the abolition of the slave trade and the suppression of the Barbary pirates. For the first, the British representative proposed a mutual right of search on the high sea. Lacking Britain's naval strength and fearing a one-sided enforcement, the continental Powers re-jected this idea, which was not to be adopted until 1831. As for the second task, Great Britain, which had already en-gaged in heavy unilateral action on the Barbary coast, was the dissenting party at Aix-la-Chapelle. She was firmly op-posed to a plan of joint action that would bring a Russian naval force into the Mediterranean.

The continental Powers would have used the Quintuple Alliance to enforce the legitimist, dynastic, divine-right principles of that "Holy Alliance" which Alexander I had announced in September 1815, but from which Britain had held contemptuously aloof. They would have imposed a system that would have choked off the liberal oppositions in Italy and Spain, checked the Latin American drive for independence, and resisted the movement of nationalities that had radiated out from the French Revolution. The England of Castlereagh and Canning, though far from lib-eral as yet in its domestic policy, refused from the first to be involved in these repressive designs. At Troppau in the autumn of 1820 and again at Laibach in the following Jan-uary, the British representatives withheld approval of Austria's decision to occupy Naples and crush the liberal opposition there. It was not until the meeting at Verona in 1822, however, that the final break came. Despite British opposition, that Congress gave its blessing to France's inter-

93

vention in Spain, a military invasion that enabled Ferdinand to defeat and decimate his constitutional opposition. This was coming too near home for a merely passive show of disapproval. The restoration of autocratic rule in Madrid was believed to threaten Portugal. It would clearly mean support of the royal resistance to independence for Spain's colonies in America. Portugal was England's "ancient ally," and British assistance to the rebellious Spanish colonies had won for British commercial interests a practical monopoly of the foreign trade of Latin America. Great Britain abandoned the Grand Alliance.

Any hope entertained in 1815 or 1818 that the Great Powers would preserve the minimum of unanimity essential for effective action in the interests of justice and peace thus proved as ill-founded as it would be in 1945. No permanent organization could unite states whose theoretical recognition of a paramount common interest in a peaceful legal order yielded at every critical point to concrete convictions of national or dynastic advantage. But the idea of a Concert of Europe was not dead. Embodied in shifting combinations of the Powers, it sustained the sporadic practice of "conference diplomacy" up to and beyond the end of the nineteenth century. Essentially a mode of *ad hoc* political adjustment, it nevertheless fostered, partly as a solution to specific problems and partly by the negotiation of multilateral conventions for general application, the development of international law.

The Hague Conventions of 1899 and 1907 included an elaborate code of arbitral procedure and provided, in the so-called Permanent Court of Arbitration, for a panel of expert and distinguished arbiters; but they made no attempt to impose arbitration or any other mode of peaceful settlement. The main subject at both Conferences was war, and the years 1914-1918 proved that abstract rules, however laboriously formulated, are powerless either to prevent war or to impose reliable restraints upon its conduct.

The political leaders who negotiated the peace treaties of 1919 and 1920 were under heavy pressure to establish international institutions that would "make the world safe for democracy." Yet they did not interpret the general consensus as one envisaging the effective subordination of the state to a universal legal order. Their League of Nations was to be an association for voluntary cooperation, not a world government. The members were to preserve their precious sovereignty. The rule of unanimity for all substantive decisions meant that any corporate authority of Council or Assembly was a function of immediate political expediencies. All that the Covenant did, then, was to provide for a machinery of settlement and enforcement that could be used if governments felt so disposed. The members did indeed undertake on paper not to resort to war until specified procedures had been tried; but when it seemed that Article 16 might *require* states to take part in sanctions enforcing this obligation, the clause was collectively "interpreted" in such a way as to allow each to decide for itself whether the occasion for police action had really presented itself. With this understood, the attempt at voluntary application against Mussolini's Italy, after beginning with a fanfare of trumpets, limped on to a shameful fiasco. The dictator blew loud and hard and "sanctions" collapsed.

The record of the League as a peace-keeping agency is a familiar tale of bright hopes, occasional small triumphs, gradual disintegration, and final collapse. This was the natural consequence of trying to achieve a revolutionary change in international relations without any change in the distribution of authority and power. A face-saving excuse, generally accepted as respectable in Europe and throughout the British Commonwealth, was found in the absence of the United States.

Within two years after the war, the basic American isolationism had reasserted itself and, like Britain in the Quintuple Alliance a century earlier, the country rejected a plan

95

of salvation of which its government had been a principal draftsman. So strong was the revulsion that no amount of tinkering with the Statute of the Permanent Court of International Justice could bring the United States even into a judicial organization that it had advocated as early as 1907. Whether the participation of its now most powerful founder might have so strengthened the League that it could have dealt successfully with the European conflicts that finally tore it apart must remain a matter of conjecture. But in the light of what has happened in the United Nations, one thing can be said with some confidence. The primary causes of the failure of world organization in the twenties and thirties lie much deeper than American aloofness during that period, and are still perilously active.

The failures of the League were so obvious and on so grand a scale that they have almost completely overshadowed the gains made under its auspices. For all its tragic disillusionments, the total experience was an advance in the direction of an effective legal order for the world. If it had done no more than expose the multiplicity and complexity of the problems of collective action on a global plane, this would have been a positive achievement. In fact it left institutions and procedures that are still in beneficent use.

The laborious attempt to codify important branches of international law, and so remove some of the uncertainties that were said to impede submission to supranational adjudication, culminated in a conference that did more to reveal than to remedy weaknesses of the existing order. On the other hand the establishment of the Permanent Court of International Justice has proved a substantial step towards the impartial interpretation and application that is a prime requisite of any legal system. The social, economic, and cultural programs directed from Geneva brought into active operation new and universal information and welfare services, paving the way for the larger and more penetrating enterprises of the United Nations in these fields. Arrangements for the protection of minorities and the development of former colonial territories marked the assumption of collective responsibility for the well-being and advancement of the less favored peoples. The spirit of human community, which is the indispensable foundation of a system of law serving the world as law serves national communities, was beginning to manifest itself in official collective institutions.

With the peace of 1945 came the second official attempt, led this time by the United States, whose refusal to join the League of Nations had always been pleaded as a principal cause of the failure of that association. The new organization was to operate by majority vote, thus, it was hoped, escaping the paralysis of unanimity. Its primary peace-keeping organ, the Security Council, was given authority, which the League had never had, to issue binding commands and, when necessary, to mobilize force to carry them out. Greatly strengthened economic, social, cultural, and health agencies were to grapple collectively with the underlying causes impeding peaceful advancement in the human community.

The text of the United Nations Charter encouraged general expectations of effective cooperation among the Great Powers in the settlement and maintenance of peace. Most of the world knew little about the stubborn debate that had gone on at San Francisco and even less about the differences as to the authority and procedures of the new Organization that were concealed rather than resolved in the formulas adopted. True, it was difficult to reconcile the privileged and dominant position granted to the five permanent members of the Security Council by Article 27 of the Charter with the "sovereign equality" stipulated in Article 2 as the first principle of the Organization. Some critics saw in this inequality a dangerous legalization of *de facto* he-

97

gemony. Such objections were met by two arguments: 1) that the burden of enforcement would necessarily fall upon the Great Powers, who must therefore have a determining voice in decisions leading to peace-keeping operations; and 2) that it would in any case be impossible to carry out such operations against the will of a Great Power. Grudgingly, the lesser states accepted this discrimination because, without it, no peace-keeping machinery would have been possible. In the event, any fear of dictation by a joint hegemony was speedily dispelled by the breakdown of the grudging wartime coalition and the resumption of irreconcilable conflict between the Communist and democratic blocs. At the same time, this brutal rebuttal of the facile assumption of unanimity among the victorious Great Powers on the essentials of peace, driven home as it was by routine Soviet resort to the veto, robbed the Security Council of the capacity to perform its prime function.

It was Russian intransigence that prevented the drafting of the agreements that Article 43 makes a condition of the use of armed force by the Security Council. As Kelsen pointed out in his early and masterly textual analysis of the Charter[2] the failure to achieve any of these agreements has rendered the Security Council powerless, quite apart from the veto, to take armed action under Article 42. The probability of long delay in the necessary negotiations was foreseen and formidable provision made for it. Pending the coming into force of a number of these agreements that the Security Council would consider sufficient to enable it "to begin the exercise of its responsibilities under Article 42," Article 106 permitted the five permanent members of the Council to take "such joint action on behalf of the Organization as may be necessary for the purpose of maintaining international peace and security." Legally speaking, this was a treaty grant to the five Powers of what Kelsen called

[2] *Iowa Law Review*, 3 (1946), 499-543.

"unrestricted dominance over the world."[3] Insofar as they can contrive to act together, the provision corresponds to the facts of international life; but the disagreement of the grantees about what to do with the world has hitherto prevented joint action under Article 106.

In his exhaustive studies of the Charter, Kelsen also revealed not only vague and confused drafting that invites radically different interpretations, but designed ambiguities. Together, these have provided commodious escape hatches from inconvenient obligations. They have also facilitated some flexible adjustments that at times have enabled the Organization to limit the range and intensity of international conflict.

Of these working arrangements, the earliest and perhaps most far-reaching was not merely a departure from the literal meaning of the text, but a violation of what was almost certainly its original intent. The general tenor of the Charter affords no grounds for qualification of the normal significance of the paragraph in Article 27 calling for "an affirmative vote of seven members including the concurring votes of the permanent members." Yet in the very first year of operation and, paradoxically enough, following the position taken by the USSR in April 1946 on the Spanish question, it was agreed that an abstention by a permanent member of the Security Council could have the same effect as a concurring vote, provided seven of the other members voted for the proposal submitted.[4] This permitted action to be taken for which there was a grudging Great-Power consensus, but of which, for reasons of their own, one or more of the permanent members did not wish to express positive approval. Abstention would be less offensive than an affirmative vote to an ally opposing the measure to be taken.

[3] *Op.cit.*, n. 19. See also H. Kelsen, *The Law of the United Nations* (London, 1950), pp. 756-61.
[4] SCOR no. 2 (1st year), p. 243; Leo Gross, "Voting in the Security Council," *Yale Law Journal*, 60 (1951), pt. 1, 212-16.

Four years later, while the Soviet seat was vacant in protest against Taiwan's continued occupation of the Chinese chair, the Council turned this concession against the USSR by treating absence as equivalent to abstention. Thus it considered itself empowered to adopt resolutions, which the Soviet representative would certainly have vetoed had he been present, mobilizing collective defense against the invasion of South Korea.

The end was admirable; the means more than dubious. To treat the abstention of an *attending* representative as a concurrent vote was in effect an informal, working amendment adopted by consent and offending the form rather than the spirit of the Charter. To take action that all must have known to be contrary to the will of an absent permanent member was to violate the consensus upon which Article 27 was founded. Nor is there any legal substance in the argument, based on Article 28.1, to the effect that the USSR had forfeited its rights by making it impossible for the Council to operate continuously in the manner prescribed.

There was an entirely constitutional alternative that would at most have delayed for some days the approval sought by the United States for action that it would in all probability have continued in any case. The Security Council could have confessed itself disqualified by the absence of a Soviet representative and called for a special session of the General Assembly under Article 20. The majority necessary for this procedural step was assured, and this was in any case what had to be done when the USSR, realizing what advantage could be taken of its absence, hastened back to the Security Council. As it was, the violent wrenching of the text gave the Kremlin an unusually substantial point for its constant charge that the Western Powers were manipulating the Charter for their own ends.

It was the shift from Council to Assembly in this case, and the repeated demonstration of American influence in the latter body, that inspired the United States to introduce in 1950 the Uniting for Peace Resolution, which passed by an overwhelming majority, opposed only by the USSR and four of its allies.[5] Contrary to a widespread opinion, this did not alter the distribution of powers and functions between the Security Council and General Assembly. Notwithstanding Soviet arguments to the contrary, Articles 11 and 14 of the Charter provide ample constitutional grounds for the kind of action that has been taken under the Resolution. It did, however, emphasize the potentialities of the General Assembly, whose recommendations, though they could call for nothing more than voluntary compliance, could nevertheless effectively implement a plan of action supported by the statutory two-thirds majority. It also provided for the swift convocation of emergency meetings of the General Assembly when the veto paralyzed the Security Council.

The same Resolution provided for a Peace Observation Commission to keep watch upon situations threatening international peace and security, and requested all members of the United Nations to earmark and maintain military forces that could be mobilized by recommendation of the Security Council or General Assembly. The arrangement was to be further fortified by a Collective Measures Committee that was to suggest ways in which the peace-keeping machinery could be strengthened, "taking account of collective self-defense and regional arrangements."

All this General Assembly superstructure could be and was defended as constitutional means of giving effect to Articles 10, 11, 12, 14, and 22 of the Charter, and the inevitable Soviet charges of flagrant breach of that instrument have been met by the constant reminder that Article 24 gives the Security Council only "primary," not exclusive, "responsibility for the maintenance of international peace

[5] Res. 377 (v).

101

and security." Nor has the USSR been above using the Resolution when it has seen national advantage in doing so. Thus in 1956 it joined in the vote for an emergency session of the General Assembly to take over action in the Suez crisis after the Security Council had been thwarted by British and French votes. The opportunity here of an appearance on the side of the angels and of simultaneously humiliating Britain and France while gaining favor with the anti-imperialists was too good to be missed. In 1958 it again voted for an emergency session, this time to deal with the situation in Lebanon and Jordan, where it was accusing the United States and United Kingdom of illegal intervention. The Assembly has frequently been called upon to deal with peace-keeping problems in which a veto has prevented the Security Council from acting; but those parts of the Resolution setting up the Peace Observation Commission and the Collective Measures Committee, as well as the appeal to members to keep forces at the disposal of the United Nations, might as well have been omitted for all their practical result. In 1951 the Commission was called upon by the General Assembly to observe the situation in the Balkans resulting from northern assistance to the Greek guerrillas but, though the membership of fourteen has been renewed from time to time, it has never been given anything further to do. The three reports submitted by the Collective Measures Committee were shelved, and states took no action on the request to maintain special forces for the United Nations.[6] The majority consensus supporting the

[6] U Thant says that the 1951 report listed units earmarked for service with the UN. Richard A. Falk and Saul H. Mendlovitz, *The Strategy of World Order*, 3: 527-28. L. M. Goodrich and A. P. Simmons, *The United Nations and the Maintenance of International Peace and Security* (Washington, D.C., 1955), pp. 427-33. William R. Frye, *A United Nations Peace Force* (Dobbs Ferry, N.Y., 1957), pp. 62-64. GAOR 1951, VI Supp. 13; GAOR 1954, Annexes, Agenda no. 19, pp. 1-4 and supp. no. 21, p. 4.

General Assembly's right and duty to find the peace threatened and to recommend corrective action did not extend to advance preparation for participation in any enforcement action that might be recommended. Upon reflection, even members enthusiastic about the confirmation of the General Assembly's powers preferred to be entirely free to decide in each case whether to contribute forces. Thus the Uniting for Peace Resolution went only a short way toward filling the gap left by the Soviet Union's rejection of all attempts in the Military Staff Committee and the Security Council to draft the agreements required by Article 43 of the Charter as a condition of any legal obligation to hold forces and facilities at the disposal of the United Nations.

The General Assembly was convoked five times in emergency session to deal with threats to the peace; but present indications are that it may not in future be so readily called upon to assume this role. The enthusiasm of the United States, strongest original advocate of the procedure, has waned with the influx of new members of varying political leanings and the resulting uncertainty of supporting majorities. As for the Soviet Union, its original opposition was renewed with fresh vigor in connection with the United Nations Operation in the Congo and, reinforced by de Gaulle's France, confronted the Organization in 1964 with the gravest crisis in its history.

The precise point in dispute since 1961 has been the liability of members to pay the General Assembly's assessments for expenses incurred in its peace-keeping activities. The Soviet Union now insists that the forces employed by the United Nations in the Middle East since the Suez crisis and in the Congo from 1960 to 1965 have been engaged in enforcement measures that belong to the exclusive competence of the Security Council; that both operations, proceeding as they have under the direction of the General Assembly, are illegal; and that the resulting expenditures are accordingly not "expenses of the Organization" to be apportioned by the General Assembly under Article 17.2. The General Assembly on December 20, 1961 asked the International Court of Justice for an advisory opinion which, handed down on July 20, 1962, held by nine votes to five that the expenses had been legally incurred in carrying out the purposes of the Organization and were therefore chargeable to all members as apportioned by the General Assembly.[7]

The advisory opinion was adopted by the General Assembly in Resolution 1854 (xvii) on December 19, 1962. The vote was 76 to 17, with 8 abstentions. The opposition included, in addition to the ussr and France, developing states concerned about their capacity to meet increases in their assessments. France was willing to pay her share in the costs of unef, having concurred in the mobilization of that force in 1956. Meanwhile, in keeping with the Gaullist turn in her foreign policy, she had come round to the Soviet view that the General Assembly had usurped functions of the Security Council, where her veto enabled her to prevent any peace-keeping measure of which she disapproved. Accordingly, she could not be persuaded to make any contribution to the costs of the Congo operation, in spite of the fact that she had not vetoed, but merely abstained from voting on, the Security Council's Resolution of July 14, 1960, instructing the Secretary-General to furnish military assistance to the government in Leopoldville.

The refusal of the ussr and France to be governed by the opinion of the International Court of Justice, approved by the General Assembly, is a telling demonstration of the relative strengths of law and national policy in the international arena. Advisory opinions are of course not binding; but they do embody the most authoritative possible statements of existing norms whether derived, as in this case,

[7] icj Reports, 1962, pp. 151-308.

from treaties, or from other sources. To disregard them is not outright defiance of the principal judicial organ of the United Nations (Charter Art. 7, and Art. 1 of the Statute of the International Court of Justice), as is the refusal to give effect to a judgment; it does, however, diminish the prestige of the tribunal, and that is a major disservice to the cause of world law.

By 1964 the USSR and nine other members were two full years in arrears in their contribution to the budget, which included UNEF and ONUC expenses.[8] Article 19 of the Charter decrees that members in this situation shall be deprived of their vote in the Assembly. There had always been some grumbling in the United States about the large share of United Nations costs that the country was called upon to bear, and Washington now decided to invoke Article 19, apparently believing that the threat of its application would induce the delinquents to reduce their arrears at least to the point of avoiding the penalty.

The USSR, repeating its argument that there was no question of arrears since expenses of peace-keeping operations not ordered by the Security Council and carried out under its direction were not legally expenses of the Organization, threatened to withdraw if its vote in the General Assembly was not recognized. It was no part of Washington's purpose to bring matters to a head-on collision that might entail a general deterioration in its relations with Russia. There was doubt as to how Article 19 could be applied, whether by the President's refusal to recognize the vote of the member in arrears or by a two-thirds majority of the Assembly. What the United States did was to insist that the Assembly could proceed to any contentious business on its agenda only if the arrears had been reduced below the penalty point or, alternatively, Article 19 had been applied. Its plan was to use the delay in negotiating for payments. The plan

[8] UNYB, 1964, pp. 3-14, 29.

105

failed, and, except for some noncontentious business transacted without vote by unanimous consent, the 1964 session of the General Assembly adjourned with nothing done. It is possible, though by no means certain, that if the United States had demanded a vote on imposing the penalty and had won the requisite majority, the USSR would have left the United Nations. It is also possible that both it and France would have paid up. What is clear is that the American effort failed both to vindicate the law of the Charter and to secure payments of which the United Nations is in dire need. Furthermore, the twentieth session of the General Assembly could only meet and transact business by a working agreement, marking the total retreat of the United States, to leave Article 19 in abeyance. Insofar as arrears contain quotas for peace-keeping activities of the General Assembly, the abeyance will probably be permanent and universal, for the precedent of 1964-1965 will be an awkward one to ignore. This means that contributions to the cost of peace-keeping operations other than those directed by the Security Council will be entirely voluntary—one more motive for abandoning all such activities to that body, where the veto will resume its full prohibitive power over the main purpose of the United Nations.

Under cover of divergent interpretations of the Charter, and of the Great-Power consensus upon which that instrument is based, the use of the Uniting for Peace Resolution has thus brought to a head a difference in political attitudes towards the Organization. One of the few things done by the nineteenth session was to provide, by unanimous consent without vote, for a Special Committee on Peace-Keeping Operations which was instructed to survey "the whole question of peace-keeping operations in all their aspects, including ways of overcoming the present financial difficulties of the Organization." The reports of this body of thirty-three members do not yet show any clear evidence that the disputants are approaching agreement on the respective constitutional roles of the Security Council and General Assembly.[9] The fact that discussions are continuing, however, is one more indication of an inclination on the part of the United States and its supporters in the argument to return to the Great-Power hegemony textually supported by Chapters 5 and 7 of the Charter. [10]

Working arrangements that diverge from a constituent text are especially vulnerable to attack when they press hard upon powerful interests. The virtuous constitutional case that can be made against them wins adherents among neutrals. But their abandonment, where that is found advisable, does not mean that they have been useless. In the Suez and Congo crises, violent disruptions of the international order were checked or prevented that might otherwise have led to general war. Whether this result could have been achieved without the United Nations is sheer conjecture. The fact that it was achieved can fairly be taken as a demonstration of the utility of that Organization. But, if this is so, it was not the only gain. The fact is that in the years that the General Assembly has been the principal organ dealing with threats to the peace, the United Nations has attained a moderating influence in world affairs that is far more general than its effect in the specific cases under treatment.

Yet the score even in concrete performance, looked at as a whole, is itself impressive. In the first year of its existence, the Security Council's watchful concern in Iran added sufficient weight to American and British pressure to secure the withdrawal of Russian troops, and enabled the Iranian

[9] *Annual Report of the Secretary-General on the Work of the Organization*, June 16, 1968-June 15, 1969, pp. 67-68.

[10] See P. Mosely's statement that the US negotiates with USSR over possible terms for restoring the decisive role of the SC, *The U.N. in the Balance*, ed. Norman J. Padelford and Leland M. Goodrich (New York, 1965), p. 308.

Government to reestablish its authority, against Soviet opposition, in Azerbaijan province. Keeping the matter on its
agenda despite the first Soviet walkout, and receiving successive appeals from Teheran, the Council was able to exercise a positive influence, acknowledged by the Iranian Government itself as a decisive factor in the recovery of its
independence.[11]

In Palestine and in Kashmir, from 1947 to the present,
conciliation commissions, mediators, and military observers
and supervisors appointed by the United Nations have ar-
ranged and supervised cease fires, truces, and armistices,
arresting open warfare in areas which continue to be bitterly contested.

In Korea, international forces under the United Nations
flag drove invading North Korean and Chinese Communist
armies, assisted though these were by the Soviet Union,
back to the thirty-eighth parallel from which they started,
and have held them there in a quarrelsome and precarious
armistice since 1953.

In 1958 Lebanon first and Jordan later complained to the
Security Council of intervention by the United Arab Republic, and appealed to the United States and United Kingdom respectively to assist in the defense of their territorial
integrity and political independence. A United Nations
Observation Group was sent to assess and possibly check
alleged infiltration of men and munitions into Lebanon; and
American troops entered that country, while a British force
was sent to Jordan. The USSR, seizing another chance to win
favor with the Arab States, charged armed intervention in
violation of the Charter, and moved that the Council demand the recall of the British and American forces. Unable
to proceed with these permanent members on different
sides, the Council unanimously decided to call an Emergency Special Session of the General Assembly. The Resolu-

[11] SCOR, ser. 1, no. 2, 30th meeting, p. 98.

tion unanimously adopted there on August 21, 1958 had, by an interesting turn of events, been concocted by ten members of the Arab League, including the two—Lebanon and Jordan—that had lodged the complaints against another member, the United Arab Republic. In the text, the General Assembly welcomed assurances that the members of the Arab League would henceforth honor their obligation not to interfere with each other's choice of regime, and called upon each member of the United Nations strictly to observe the principles of respect for the territorial integrity and political independence of other members and of nonintervention in their internal affairs. It went on to instruct the Secretary-General to make practical arrangements facilitating withdrawal of foreign troops from Lebanon and Jordan. This combination of an Arab promise of good behavior and an exhortation to all members to remember their vows, plus the Observation Group's report that it had found no evidence of serious infiltration, paved the way for American and British retreat from an internationally unpopular enterprise and for a lull in complaints and recriminations. The proceedings were another demonstration of the utility of a standing chamber for parliamentary diplomacy on a universal scale.

When the long Middle Eastern conflict exploded into the Suez crisis of 1956, the Organization played an indispensable role in arresting hostilities that threatened to expand into major war, and its Emergency Force was employed there until 1967 in keeping an uneasy peace between Israel and the United Arab Republic.

In the Congo, forces voluntarily contributed by members and organized by the Secretary-General under instructions from the Security Council facilitated Belgian withdrawal and the ouster of foreign mercenaries, while United Nations diplomacy averted what might well have been a violent collision of the USSR and Western Powers in a strug-

109

gle for dominating influence there. Hardly less important in the tremendous task of welding together a much divided population and laying the foundations of stable, independent nationhood was the technical assistance devotedly rendered by United Nations agencies in the organization of medical, educational, and other social services and the reconstruction of government and industry on national lines. In this instance, the financial straits of the United Nations have compelled termination of military aid and curtailment of technical assistance at a point where the viability of the new state is anything but secure.

Undisputed credit went to the United Nations again for its constructive part in working out conditions that resolved the Cuban missile crisis of 1962. While it cannot compel its strongest members to drop their differences in a common effort for peace, it proved in this instance its ability to exercise a mediating influence in a most dangerous confrontation. Three years later, in the Dominican Republic, the Secretary-General and his representative foreshadowed the role that the Organization may yet regularly play in coping with the complex problems of revolution and intervention.

In Cyprus, since March 1964, the United Nations has succeeded in holding Greek and Turkish interventions in support of the Greek majority and Turkish minority short of war between the two states, while forces again organized by the Secretary-General under instructions from the Security Council have checked the internecine slaughter on the island.

It would be remiss to leave the peace-keeping efforts of the United Nations without touching upon the unexpected development of the Secretary-General's part therein. A comparison of Article 6 of the Covenant of the League of Nations and Articles 7, 97-100 of the United Nations Charter makes it clear enough, even without the record of the San Francisco Conference, that the founding fathers of

1945 intended to give the Secretary-General a measure of responsibility and initiative that had not formally belonged to his prototype in the League. Even in the League, experience proved that anything approaching efficient administration involved proposals, personal interventions, consultations, and decisions that partook of the political character. Even that most conservative and correct of international civil servants, Sir Eric Drummond, afterward Earl of Perth, had occasionally to step out of the purely administrative role, if there is such a thing.[12] What those draftsmen of the Charter who had been active in the League probably had in mind was an official somewhere between Sir Eric Drummond and Albert Thomas, the dynamic and irrepressible Director of the International Labor Office. They probably little realized the leeway they were offering a man of subtle mind and determined purpose.

The first Secretary-General, Trygve Lie, a former Cabinet Minister in Norway, began developing the potentialities of the office in a way that brought him into conflict with the USSR. His successor, Dag Hammarskjöld, a high civil servant in Sweden, son of a former prime minister and brother of a former judge of the Permanent Court of International Justice, followed the same course with less bluntness and more finesse up to its climax in the Congo operation. There, beginning in July 1960, the Secretary-General, responding to a plea from the president and the prime minister of the Congo (Leopoldville) for United Nations military assistance against what they called foreign aggression, wrote his own ticket, had it confirmed by the Security Council *without Soviet objection*, and proceeded to organize and command, under instructions drafted by himself, military and relief operations, technical assistance, and United Nations relations with successive Congolese governments. All of this

[12] Cf. F. P. Walters, *A History of the League of Nations* (London and New York, 1952), pp. 393-94, 558-59, and *passim*.

had an irreproachable legal basis in the combination of Charter Articles 98 and 99, and constituted an efficient way of meeting the new state's complex requirements of external assistance. Unfortunately the program soon clashed with Soviet national designs in the Congo, at which point the Kremlin, classifying Mr. Hammarskjöld out of hand as a tool of "the capitalist-imperialist conspiracy," not only repudiated his direction of ONUC but proposed the famous *troika*. This would have converted the secretary-generalship into a triumvirate representing each of the three main groups of states—Communist, uncommitted, and capitalist. The practical result would have been a Soviet veto on every exercise of the Secretary-General's functions. Happily the plan, which would have gravely impeded United Nations action, won little support. But the Soviet Union's refusal thenceforward to recognize Mr. Hammarskjöld as Secretary-General, and its insistence that the Congo operation was an illegally conducted enterprise to the costs of which members were under no obligation to contribute, produced much of the desired effect. At least until Moscow seriously espouses the purposes of the United Nations, the Secretary-General will be well advised to use the powers of his office with great restraint.

Many critics have deplored the multiplication of weak members, each with a vote in the General Assembly formally equal to that of the most powerful. This is said to institutionalize a divorce of authority from capacity and contribution. The same can be said of universal adult suffrage. Some even describe it as a divorce of authority and responsibility, though the greater members have not evinced any remarkable sense of responsibility for the fulfillment of Charter obligations.

What the record seems rather to indicate is that formal equality in the General Assembly has heightened the appeal of that body as a permanent agency of conciliation and adjustment to which there is now an established habit of recourse. For weaker states especially, we should expect palpable advantage in bringing grievances to a public forum rather than to a private negotiation in which they have not the psychological and moral support of others with similar problems and a similar inferiority of material strength. In not a few instances this has proved true of the United Nations. At the very least, the applicant with something more than a merely captious complaint has had a sympathetic hearing and a serious examination of his brief. More than that, such suits as those of Iran against the USSR in 1946, Burma against the Republic of China (Taiwan) in 1953-54, Greece against the United Kingdom concerning the independence of Cyprus, 1954-1959, and Morocco and Tunisia against France, 1951-1961, have proved that the proceedings may persuade even a Great Power to make concessions to a weaker people. The General Assembly, in particular, returning year after year to the attack, has shown a pertinacity that wears down resistance. The possessor's complacent belief that greatness is rectitude is becoming more difficult to sustain under that body's informed and persistent probing.

Not that the record is by any means consistent. The United Nations could do nothing for Hungary against the Soviet Union, though it kept up the effort for six years. Guatemala, Cuba, and the Dominican Republic have made little headway in Security Council or General Assembly against the United States plea of prior jurisdiction in the Organization of American States, where Washington is still confident of a majority, as it formerly was in the United Nations. These cases remind us that when "vital" interests are at stake, relative power is still the determining factor.

Twenty years after the drafting of the Covenant, the League of Nations disintegrated under the onslaught of the Second World War. Twenty-one years after the United Na-

113

tions came into operation, that Organization, by suspending the application of Article 19 of its Charter, was able to survive a crisis that threatened to tear it apart. Its survival reflects a widespread official conviction of something more than merely marginal utility. Yet that it is still far from the center of gravity in world affairs is attested by its refusal to deal with the conflict in Vietnam, and by the inability of the permanent members of the Security Council, even with the resources of Article 106 at their disposal, to stop the Arab-Israeli War.

Anyone who hopes for the eventual transformation of the state into a disciplined unit of government under supranational authority will find in what precedes a formidable array of counterindications. These realities, which are coeval with human history, and which have thus far proved invulnerable to attack, have persuaded not only politicians but also many sophisticated political scientists to accept the international system as something fixed in any given epoch by forces that defy and will continue to defy unified control. At most this school of thought would concede the possibility of world empire; but this, like past attempts at it, would be at best a partial, temporary, and imperfect domination. Anything in the nature of a democratic federation of the world's peoples is dismissed as sheer illusion.

This negative position seems to me to ignore a positive trend in the story of mankind. Since the dawn of history political communities have been expanding geographically and ethnically, spreading the net of more or less effective authority over diversified areas and over peoples of disparate cultures. What Aristotle considered the ideal commonwealth, with its maximum population of ten thousand in an area small enough to permit immediate communication by the means available in his day, has become a small town under local administration, subject, like hundreds or thousands of the like, to a common national government. If

the original mode of expansion was conquest or coloniza-
tion, this has now given way to voluntary association
planned to meet common needs. Why the process should
stop short with the present constellation of nation states is
by no means clear. Indeed, the now constant groping towards larger integration for purposes ranging from security to health and prosperity, impeded as it is by sacrosanct
myths and special interests, suggests forces moving men
willy-nilly towards universal organization.

The fragmentation of old empires in Africa and Asia was
brought about by a passion for independent nationhood
which on the surface belies the trend. If, however, there is
to be a larger integration, this was a necessary preparation
for it. The nationalism that broke up the empires was
largely a demand for formal equality in place of subjuga-
tion or condescension, and the peoples who with the assistance of the United Nations won that struggle are not only
already seeking new regional organization but joining in
their recourse to the United Nations for the solution of the
myriad problems with which their new sovereignties cannot unilaterally cope.

The United Nations itself, whose primary peace-keeping
structure assumed the unanimity of the Great Powers, has
shown a flexibility that has enabled it, despite their chronic
animosity, to resolve or materially assist in resolving a number of critical conflicts. Clearly the gravest crises in world
politics are not overcome by direct action of the Security
Council or General Assembly; but in these bodies the pressures of worldwide concern are brought to bear upon
parties in conflict and the influences making for peaceful adjustment are reinforced. At the same time, the economic
and social agencies associated with the United Nations
demonstrate the benefits of expertly guided cooperation in
agricultural, industrial, and commercial development and
in educational and welfare services. Remote as it still is

115

from effective world government, the growing complex of international institutions constitutes an impressive expression and implementation of a growing sense of human community.

Meanwhile in Europe, historically most warlike of continents, an economic and political integration has taken place that should stand as a warning to those who proclaim the nation-state to be the final achievement in centralized authority. Checked momentarily by an explosion of atavistic egocentrism touched off in France by General de Gaulle, the movement toward unity in Western Europe has already advanced far beyond anything that the Pan-Europeans of thirty years ago would have thought possible. Reasoned response to common needs has in twelve years produced there a law, structure, and practice of cooperation that sets the pace for regional organization everywhere.

5.

REGIONAL ORGANIZATION[1]

THE ORGANIZATION OF AMERICAN STATES

Supranational organization on a regional scale has become very much the fashion since the end of the Second World War in 1945. Until that time, the only intergovernmental regional association with a general program of security and welfare was the Union of American Republics. With the Pan-American Union in Washington as its central secretariat and administrative office, and specialized agencies quartered in various American capitals, the Union of American Republics had a panoply of overlapping conferences, congresses, councils, committees, bureaus, and institutes skirmishing with problems of security, the pacific settlement of disputes, commercial, industrial and cultural development, health, education, human rights, labor relations,

[1] This chapter discusses what I take to be the type of regional organization contemplated in Articles 52-54 of the UN Charter. I have always taken the view, expounded with his habitual cogency by Julius Stone in *Legal Controls of International Conflict* (New York, 1954), pp. 247-251, that this does not include such defensive alliances as those established by the Brussels Treaty of 1948, the North Atlantic Treaty of 1949, the Warsaw Pact of 1955, the Southeast Asia Collective Defense Treaty of 1954, or the Baghdad Pact of 1955. These were designed to meet the failure, revealed after 1945, of the Charter's security system as a restraint upon the Great Powers. For their conformity with the Charter the parties rely upon the collective defense provision of Article 51, not upon Articles 52-54. For a concise statement of this interpretation see my *Law and Society in the Relations of States* (New York, 1951), pp. 270-71.

117

social progress, and international legal codes for the Americas.

Although its remote beginnings go back to the Conference of Panama in 1826, and its more or less continuous operation to the Washington Conference of 1889, all this co-operative activity had no overall constitutional structure until 1951, when the Charter drawn up at Bogota in 1948 came into force. Its congeries of specialized agencies and its series of general and special conferences depended upon a wide variety of acts, some of them treaties, some mere resolutions. There was a widespread belief that strength and efficiency could be gained from a unifying constitution distributing function and authority, and by 1928 this belief was strong enough to secure adoption at Havana of a draft convention prepared by the Commission of Jurists which, since its establishment at Rio de Janeiro in 1906, had been the inter-American body specifically concerned with the development and formulation of international codes for the Americas. This draft constitution suffered the fate of many other products of the periodic conferences—failure to obtain the ratifications necessary to bring it into force. It is some indication of a strengthening sense of community that the Bogota Charter, drafted twenty years later, came into force in 1951, when two-thirds of the signatories had ratified it, and that by 1956 it had been accepted by all twenty-one republics.

The duty of all members to assist in case of armed attack upon any American states and the method of organizing collective action in such an event had already been laid down in the Rio Treaty of 1947, which is taken up into the Bogota Charter by Article 25. By Article 2 of the same Treaty, the parties had also bound themselves "to submit every controversy which may arise between them to methods of peaceful settlement." The substance of this is expanded into Articles 20-23 of the Bogota Charter, and the various permissible methods of settlement are elaborated in the monumental Pact of Bogota drawn up at the same Conference. This Pact has come into force between only ten states. For them it replaces the whole complex of previous inter-American agreements on conciliation and arbitration, adding the new obligation, when other methods fail, of submitting the dispute, at the request of any party, to the International Court of Justice. For all those members of oas that have not ratified the Pact of Bogota, the obligation and methods of settlement are to be found in the Rio Treaty of 1947, the Bogota Charter of 1948, and earlier instruments, of which the most elaborate are the Conciliation and Arbitration Conventions concluded in Washington between December 1928 and January 1929.

At first sight, the obligation of peaceful settlement looks all-inclusive. The stipulation in Article 2 of the Rio Treaty is repeated in Article 20 of the Bogota Charter. But Article 22 of the Charter limits the obligation to disputes which, in the opinion of any disputant, cannot be settled through the usual diplomatic channels," which seems to leave submission very much to the discretion of any state involved. The scope of the undertaking is still further narrowed when we turn to the Bogota Pact. Here we find not only the familiar exception of disputes on matters within the domestic jurisdiction (Art. 5), but the further exclusion of controversies concerning the protection of nationals "when the said nationals have had available means to place their case before competent domestic courts" (Art. 7). This latter proviso is broader than the general international-law condition of exhaustion of local remedies if, regardless of the character or outcome of proceedings actually available, it may be interpreted as excluding a complaint of denial of justice. The domestic-jurisdiction exception is controlled, in the text of the Pact, if a case eventually reaches the International Court of Justice, by the jurisdiction given to the Court

(Art. 38) to rule upon it. This Article, however, was the object of reservations by several signatories, including the United States, which insists here, as in its 1946 "acceptance" of the Court's jurisdiction, on its own definition of "domestic."

Similarly, the mutual security system created by the Rio Treaty and the Bogota Charter is subject to one drastic limitation. The Organ of Consultation is empowered to decide upon collective measures, in the event of attack upon an American state, by a two-thirds majority. There is here no such veto as has so often paralyzed the Security Council of the United Nations. But no member of the OAS is obliged to use armed force.[2] Collective armed action cannot be commanded by any inter-American authority.

Peaceful settlement and the control of violence are separable in theory but much intermingled in practice. They require distinct machinery, but certainly in the Inter-American system the machinery designed to prevent or check aggression and intervention has usually operated in a conciliatory rather than a compulsory capacity. Only three times have sanctions been ordered or recommended by the Council or the Meeting of Foreign Ministers acting as Organ of Consultation.

Under Trujillo's dictatorship the Dominican Republic was a chronic troublemaker, harboring and supporting foreign left-wing rebels plotting to overthrow their national governments, while these governments in turn, concerned about the dictator's disregard for human rights and alarmed at his aggressive interventions, supported exiles organizing against him. In 1949 and 1950 Haiti had twice appealed to the Council of the OAS charging official Dominican implication in armed plots to oust the Haitian Government. The Council, acting under Rio Article 6, called a Meeting of the Foreign Ministers, which is the regular

[2] Rio Treaty, Arts. 17 and 20.

120

Organ of Consultation in situations threatening the peace of America, but without naming place or date. Thus, employing tactics already used with some success in an earlier dispute between Costa Rica and Nicaragua, it took advantage of Article 12 of the Rio Treaty, which empowered it to act as Provisional Organ of Consultation pending the Meeting of Foreign Ministers. Keeping in its own hands a conflict which could hardly be regarded as having reached a stage calling for collective measures of coercion and employing investigating and supervisory commissions as well as the Inter-American Peace Committee, the Council was able to maintain a measure of restraint upon the parties. In a word, it acted, as it has in later troubles, as a standing agency of conciliation. In 1960, however, when Venezuela accused the Trujillo government of connivance and material support in an attempt to assassinate President Betancourt, the Council found the situation threatening enough to summon a Meeting of Foreign Ministers at San José, which for the first time imposed sanctions. Acting under Rio Articles 6 and 8, the foreign ministers ordered an immediate break in diplomatic relations with the Dominican Republic and a partial economic boycott. Trujillo having been assassinated in May 1961, these sanctions were terminated in January 1963, on assurances from the Dominican government then in power that the conditions calling for their imposition no longer existed.

By 1962 the center of alarm had shifted to Cuba, where Castro was dramatically flouting the Inter-American interdiction of "international Communism." In January, the Eighth Meeting of Consultation of Foreign Ministers not only ordered suspension of trade in war materials with Cuba, but applied a sanction not provided for in any of the constituent instruments, namely exclusion of the Castro government from participation in the Inter-American system. On March 23, 1962, the Security Council of the United

121

Nations had before it a draft resolution submitted by Cuba asking for an advisory opinion from the International Court of Justice on the question whether this exclusion constituted regional enforcement requiring authorization by the Security Council. This got only two votes, those of the USSR and Rumania. Chile, China, France, Ireland, the United Kingdom, the United States, and Venezuela voted against it, while the United Arab Republic abstained and Ghana did not participate.

These decisions were designed to combat the spread of Communism in the hemisphere—a peril to the democracy and human rights to which all the American states declared themselves devoted and one against which conferences in 1948, 1951, and 1954 had already attempted to inspire collective defense. On October 23, at the height of the missile crisis that climaxed Soviet intervention in American affairs, the OAS Council, again going through the form of convoking a Meeting of the Foreign Ministers without date or place, but itself taking the necessary immediate action, as Provisional Organ of Consultation under Rio Article 12, found that "the Government of Cuba, despite repeated warnings, has secretly endangered the peace of the continent by permitting the Sino-Soviet powers to have intermediate and middle range missiles on its territory capable of carrying nuclear warheads." On this finding, it resolved "to call for the immediate dismantling and withdrawal from Cuba of all missiles and other weapons with any offensive capability, and to recommend that the member states . . . take all measures, individual and collective, including the use of armed force, which they may deem necessary to insure that the Government of Cuba cannot continue to receive from the Sino-Soviet powers military material and related supplies which may threaten the peace and security of the Continent." This Resolution of course enabled the United

122

States to characterize the "quarantine," upon which it had already unilaterally decided, as a mandate of the OAS.

The action taken by the Tenth Meeting of Consultation of Ministers of Foreign Affairs on May 6, 1965, when, to cope with the sanguinary civil strife in the Dominican Republic, it requested "member states that are willing and capable of doing so to make contingents of their land, naval, air or police forces available to the OAS . . . to form an inter-American force that will operate under the authority of this Tenth Meeting of Consultation," is hardly to be classified as sanction. The Resolution stipulated "that this force will have as its sole purpose, in a spirit of democratic impartiality, that of cooperating in the restoration of normal conditions in the Dominican Republic, in maintaining the security of its inhabitants and the inviolability of human rights, and in the establishment of an atmosphere of peace and conciliation that will permit the functioning of democratic institutions." Again the effect was to clothe in the mantle of collective action the swift and unilateral military intervention of the United States, and the decision obtained only the bare two-thirds vote necessary for passage. The mainspring of Washington's action was again the fear of Soviet Communist encroachment—a fear clearly shared by many of the Latin American states. But a highly important minority voted against the Resolution (Chile, Ecuador, Mexico, Peru, and Uruguay) while Venezuela abstained. This was an expression of that long-standing aversion to interference by the "colossus of the North" which has been one of the stronger bonds of union among the Latin American states and the reason for repeated prohibitions of intervention "for any reason whatever" in their internal or external affairs.[3] Even collective intervention is still abhorred by

[3] See e.g., the Montevideo Convention of 1933 on the Rights and Duties of States, Art. 8; the Buenos Aires Protocol of 1936 on Non-Intervention, Art. 1; and the Bogota Charter of 1948, Art. 15.

123

some members, especially if it is to be supported by joint forces. In its present effort to strengthen the OAS, partly by provision for military units readily available for collective use, the United States is meeting determined opposition. The Protocol of Amendment adopted by the Third Special Inter-American Conference at Buenos Aires on February 27, 1967, which is to come into force for ratifying states when it has been ratified by two-thirds of the signatories to the Bogota Charter, makes no such provision. The inadequacy of the hemisphere's existing security system, and the failure of the amendments to remedy its defects, were made the subject of a recorded statement by the Delegation of Argentina on signing the Protocol.

The Inter-American Peace Committee

The Second Meeting of Consultation of Foreign Ministers at Havana in 1940 made provision for an Inter-American Peace Committee. Under its 1950 statute this body, consisting of representatives of five member states designated for five-year terms by the Council of the OAS, could "take action at the request of any American State, when the recourse of direct negotiations has been exhausted, when none of the other customary procedures of diplomacy or of pacific settlement is in process or when existing circumstances render negotiation impracticable." If the request came from a state directly interested in a dispute, action did not depend upon consent of the other or others. In 1956 a revised statute limited the Committee's operation to cases where all parties consented, and the Bogota Protocol of Amendment (1967) retains this limitation (Arts. 83-89) upon the work of what is to be known as the Inter-American Committee on Peaceful Settlement. Even where the consent of all parties is forthcoming, the function of the Committee is limited to good offices, fact-finding, report, and recommendation. It does not arbitrate and has no powers of enforcement. Despite these weaknesses, the Committee has been able to render substantial services, especially in the Caribbean area, where it has been repeatedly called upon by member states to establish facts and make recommendations for settling disputes.

Human Rights

The Inter-American Commission on Human Rights was created by Resolution VIII of the Fifth Meeting of Consultation of Ministers of Foreign Affairs at Santiago, Chile, in August 1959. It is made up of seven persons "elected, as individuals, by the Council of the Organization of American States from panels of three names presented by the Governments." The same Resolution instructed the Inter-American Council of Jurists to prepare a draft convention on human rights. Pending the coming into force of this convention, the Commission was to be guided by the standards formulated at Bogotá, May 2, 1948, in the American Declaration on the Rights and Duties of Man. This Declaration contains most of the principles enunciated in December of the same year by the General Assembly of the United Nations in its Universal Declaration of Human Rights.

The statute which in 1960 defined the powers and procedures of the Commission failed to give it any authority to consider private communications or to make recommendations to specific governments. Its studies, reports, requests for information, and recommendations were to be addressed to the governments in general. In practice, however, it repeatedly did employ both these methods of promoting human rights, and this liberal interpretation of its functions was acquiesced in by all the states concerned except Cuba. Repeatedly between 1960 and 1965 it examined denunciations of abuses from individuals and groups in the Dominican Republic, Cuba, Haiti, Ecuador, Guatemala, Honduras, Nicaragua, and Paraguay, and addressed its observations to their governments. Missions were sent to the Dominican Republic and to Paraguay to examine conditions on the spot and confer with the authorities. Only Cuba and Haiti definitely refused to receive such missions. In the revised statutes of 1965, the Commission is explicitly empowered to engage in the kind of direct relations with governments which it had in fact inaugurated, a confirmation attesting genuine concern for the protection of the individual against arbitrary power and some actual progress in that direction.

The draft convention prepared by the Council of Jurists contained the plan for an Inter-American Court of Human Rights. As in Europe, such a tribunal would greatly strengthen the hand of the Commission. The draft has never been submitted for adoption by an Inter-American Conference, and there is a strong movement now against a regional convention, and a general tendency to regard the United Nations Covenants as an adequate codification for the Americas. If this position is finally taken by the Organization of American States, there is still the possibility of regional institutions of interpretation and enforcement.[4]

The OAS and the Development and Codification of International Law

The development and codification of an international law of the Americas had been an objective of various Latin American congresses even before the First Inter-American

[4] See Reports on the Sessions of the Inter-American Commission on Human Rights, esp. 8th, 12th, 16th, 17th, and 18th Sessions. For recent surveys of its work, see Inter-American Institute of International Legal Studies, *The Inter-American System, Its Development and Strengthening* (Dobbs Ferry, N.Y., 1966), pp. 39-68; L. R. Schuman, "The Inter-American Commission on Human Rights," AJIL, 59 (1965), 335-344; J. A. Cabranes, "The Protection of Human Rights by the Organization of American States," AJIL, 62 (1958), 889-908.

Conference in 1889. The Second Conference, at Mexico City in 1901-1902, adopted a draft treaty to establish a Commission of Jurists that would undertake the preparation of the necessary conventions on behalf of all the American Republics. This draft failed to attract the ratifications necessary to bring it into effect. The next Conference, at Rio de Janiero in 1906, was more successful. Seventeen of the Republics ratified the convention there adopted, and the Committee, consisting of one member for each ratifying state, was able to hold its first meeting in 1912. The membership was doubled by a Resolution of the Fifth Conference, held at Santiago in 1923.[5] This body produced no less than twelve drafts for the Sixth Conference at Havana in 1928, and eleven of these were eventually approved and submitted to the states for ratification. One of the eleven was the Bustamante Code of Private International Law formulating uniform rules for the conflict of laws, a very useful beginning, ratified by fifteen states, of a movement of unification which is still in progress. Another was the draft constitution which, as we have seen, remained a dead letter for want of adequate ratification. A third came into force as the Havana Convention on the Rights and Duties of States in the Event of Civil Strife, to be flouted repeatedly in successive Caribbean disputes, and never more flamboyantly or disastrously than by the United States in the Bay of Pigs invasion of 1961. The Conference also adopted conventions on diplomatic and consular relations, asylum, the status of aliens, the rights of neutrals in maritime war, treaties, copyright, and civil aviation. The Convention on Civil Aviation incorporated the principles of the Convention of Paris of 1919 to which only five American states, not including the United States, were parties. This Convention was ratified by eleven states, but subsequently

[5] J. B. Scott, ed., *International Conferences of American States, 1889-1928* (New York, 1931), pp. 144-146, 245-247.

denounced by the United States, Chile, Dominican Republic, Guatemala, and Mexico.

Thus far the record is no more hit-and-miss than that of other international organizations. None of the conventions listed above has been ratified by all the American states. Only six ratified the Copyright Convention, only eight that on treaties. Uniformity of position on the subjects dealt with has rarely been achieved. Divergencies have indeed become more marked. The products of the Montevideo Conference of 1933, which adopted conventions on the nationality of women, on nationality in general, on extradition, on political asylum, and on the rights and duties of states, have found less acceptance, with the exception of the last-mentioned, than those of 1928. The treaty that came nearest to universal American adoption of those concluded up to 1933 was not a direct product of the inter-American organization, but of the Argentine Government, and it was open to ratification by non-American states. That was the Anti-War Treaty of Non-Aggression and Conciliation, signed at Rio de Janeiro in 1933 and ratified by all the Republics except Bolivia. The legislative record of the oas, in a word, is hardly less one of discord than of solidarity. It nevertheless bears witness to a persistent interest in international law and an invincible belief in the advantages to be gained by clarifying and strengthening it.

Unfortunately, as it has been organized since 1948, the inter-American arrangements for this work have become more complex, dilatory, and inefficient. The Bogota Charter divided the legal establishment of the oas into the Inter-American Council of Jurists, composed of representatives of all member states—a body more political than expert—and made the Inter-American Juridical Committee, consisting of nine jurists, the permanent committee of this Council (Arts. 57, 59, 67-72). Progress under the new dispensation has been lamentably slow. The drafts laboriously prepared by the Committee run into opposition in the Council and are referred back for further study. Alwyn Freeman reports that in the sixteen years from 1948 to 1964, two conventions on asylum adopted at Caracas in 1954 are the only products of Council and Committee that have come into force.[6] A draft convention on human rights, and another on extradition, were prepared for submission to the Eleventh Conference of American States, scheduled since 1954 to meet in Quito, but still postponed pending relaxation of boundary tensions between Ecuador and Peru.

Repeated attempts to draft an agreed statement of rules to govern the recognition of new governments have been defeated by the opposition of a number of the Republics, including the United States, to making recognition conditional upon the assurance of democratic procedures and the protection of human rights.

There are new signs of a feeling that in the development of international law the OAS can add little if anything to the work of the United Nations. It is significant that in some matters referred to it for codification, the Committee held that it could not do better than recommend that the American states accede to general conventions concluded under the auspices of the United Nations.[7] Furthermore, proposals to establish an Inter-American Court of Justice have met with the objection that such a step might weaken the International Court of Justice.[8]

Economic Development

From its very beginning in 1889, the association of American states has had as a principal objective the development

[6] *Proceedings of the American Society of International Law*, 1965, p. 18. The Inter-American Bank Agreement of 1959, ratified by all members except Cuba, is a creation of the Economic and Social Council.

[7] Freeman, *loc.cit.*, p. 20.

[8] *Annals of the* OAS, 1949, 51-52; Thomas and Thomas, in the work cited in n. 9 below, p. 290.

of more profitable economic relations among its members. What has been known since 1910 as the Pan-American Union was set up at the Washington Conference of 1889 as the "Commercial Bureau of the American Republics," and this agency has been the center of the most systematic and sustained activity of the association. From a commercial bureau gathering and communicating economic statistics and preparing the way for agreements aimed at the simplification of customs formalities and the unification of laws on patents, trade marks, shipping, and consular practice, it has broadened out into a general secretariat with departments corresponding to the multifarious fields in which the Organization of American States has attempted, with success by no means commensurate with the magnitude of its plans, to serve the asserted common interests of its members.

In the Second World War the meetings of the ministers of foreign affairs, and the Financial and Economic Advisory Committee which they established, facilitated the procurement of military equipment and supplies, and helped to find American markets for commodities deprived by the war of European outlets. But the United States, initiator of most of the Organization's activity, long opposed any permanent organization to rationalize production and exchange and to finance development. The marked change which has made it now the driving advocate of such organization may be dated from 1959, when it dropped its opposition to the plan for an Inter-American Development Bank, and provided the capital necessary to bring that agency into operation in 1959.

The inauguration of the "Alliance for Progress" at a special meeting of the Economic and Social Council at Punta del Este in August 1961 was to some extent an effort of the United States to counteract the odium and apprehension created by the ill-fated Bay of Pigs invasion. It was, however, an expansion of "Operation Pan-America" which the Eisenhower Administration had already been fostering, and the undertaking to provide more than half the twenty-billion-dollar capital contemplated as the minimum needed for ten years of operation expressed what was at once a generous and a prudent determination to promote economic development, social welfare, and democratic government in Latin America. The results of the first seven years of the Alliance are almost everywhere regarded as disappointing. The vastness of the obstacles to systematic modernization in a continent where the average level of illiteracy is thirty percent or more, where agricultural production is held down by a feudal type of landholding and primitive methods of cultivation, and where industry is paralyzed by lack of investment capital and by erratic fiscal policies, is only beginning to be realized. Yet the enterprise cannot be written off as wasted effort. In a number of countries, there are palpable signs of improvement and cogent evidence of a new resolution to effect drastic reforms on the part of their governments. The improvement has been sufficient to stimulate a new drive, led by the United States, to strengthen the OAS not only as a hemispheric mechanism for maintaining internal peace and security from external aggression, but as an instrument of economic, social, and political reform. An immediate objective is nothing less than an Inter-American Common Market to link up and generalize such existing institutions as the Central American Common Market and the halting ten-state Free Trade Association. These projects were on the agenda of the Conference of American Presidents held at Punta del Este in April 1967.[9]

[9] DSB, May 8, 1967, pp. 706-721. For independent assessments of the OAS and the Alliance for Progress, see A.V.W. Thomas and A. J. Thomas, Jr., *The Organization of American States* (Dallas, Tex., 1963); John C. Dreier, *The Organization of American States and*

REGIONAL ORGANIZATION IN WESTERN EUROPE

Short of federal union, the highest degree of supranational integration, not only on paper but in actual practice, has been achieved in the three so-called Communities—European Coal and Steel (CECA), European Economic (CEE, popularly known as the Common Market), and European Atomic Energy (Euratom)—and in the European Commission and Court of Human Rights created by the Rome Convention of 1950. The membership of the Communities hitherto has been confined to "the Six"—France, Italy, West Germany, Belgium, The Netherlands, and Luxembourg—while the human rights organization includes sixteen states. In all four cases, prerogatives traditionally exercised exclusively by states have been handed over to supranational authorities.

The Communities

Thus, the High Authority of CECA, consisting of nine persons elected not as representatives of states but as technical experts, may by majority adopt decisions binding upon all members of the Community, while the Council of Ministers (one member of government from each state), acting on a finding by the High Authority, may by a two-thirds vote impose penalties upon states failing to comply with treaty provisions.[10]

The treaty concluded in 1954 to form a European Defense Community was rejected by the French parliament and never came into force. In the interval since 1951 a strong current of French resistance to the movement toward Western European integration had set in, a resistance

---

Hemisphere Crisis (New York, 1962); Gordon Connell-Smith, *The Inter-American System* (London and New York, 1966); and T. J. Draper, "The Alliance for Progress: Failures and Opportunities," in *Yale Review,* LV (December 1965), pp. 182-190.

[10] CECA Treaty, 1951, Arts. 9, 13, 14, 88.

that grew in obstinacy under President de Gaulle. This goes far to explain the fact that the 1957 treaty creating CEE did not give to its Commission and Council, or indeed to the Court of Justice that serves all three Communities, powers quite equal to those conferred by the CECA Treaty of 1951. True, decisions of the Council or Commission imposing pecuniary obligations upon persons other than states are given executory force in each state member's territory, which means that they are enforceable there on application to the appropriate national authority (Art. 192). But when a state is held to be violating the treaty, the collective decision can only call upon it to comply and, if it refuses, summon it before the Court of Justice. Formally, the state is bound by the Court's decision; but there is no authority here to impose sanctions (Arts. 169-171). And, whereas Article 89 of the CECA Treaty gives jurisdiction to the Court in any dispute between member states as to the application of the treaty, and allows proceedings to be instituted by the request of one party, Article 182 of the CEE Treaty makes jurisdiction conditional upon a compromis.

The Court of Justice has general jurisdiction to hear complaints lodged against member states by other members or by the administrative authorities of the Communities, and in complaints against those authorities by member states or by private persons or enterprises. It does not hear cases brought directly against states by private persons or enterprises. These may be taken to national courts which are bound to apply treaty law, or to the administrative authority of the relevant Community whence they may indirectly reach the Court.

Standing formally at the head of all this organization is the body of one hundred and forty-two deputies somewhat euphemistically styled the "European Parliament." Modelled upon the Common Assembly of the Coal and Steel Community, it now "advises and supervises" all three Communities. In the Rome Treaty of 1957 (Articles 137-144) it retained the title "Assembly"; but, in what has thus far proved an abortive effort to enhance its dignity and authority, its members substituted the present name in March 1962 over French opposition.

Limited by Article 137 to "advisory and supervisory powers," its composition and mode of election were fixed by the next Article: "The Assembly shall consist of delegates who shall be nominated by the respective Parliaments from among their members," thirty-six each for France, Germany, and Italy, fourteen each for Belgium and The Netherlands, and six for Luxembourg. The proposal to elect it by direct universal suffrage, and thus give it more of the character of a body representing the people of Europe rather than their separate national parliaments, was postponed *sine die* at the constituent conference of 1957. Nominally the compromise was temporary, for paragraph 3 of Article 138 called upon the Assembly to "draw up proposals for election by direct universal suffrage." In reality the treaty in no way commits the parties to the creation of a true European parliament, for only the Council, composed of ministers of the states members, can decide how and when the transformation is to take place, and then only by unanimous vote. Meanwhile, the so-called Parliament has neither legislative nor budgetary powers. Its influence upon the policies of the Communities depends upon the studies and reports of its numerous committees, the procedure of question and answer at its sessions, and such advocacy as its deputies may undertake in their respective legislatures.

In operation, the European Communities constitute a delicate and uneasy compromise between a federation and a mere association of sovereign states. Under the energetic leadership of President Hallstein, the Commission of the Economic Community embodied the active federal principle, hitherto checked in the Council of Ministers, where

France leads the opposition to any invasions of national sovereignty beyond those explicitly ordained by the treaty. The obstructionist power of any one member state might have been expected to come to an end when on January 1, 1966, under the terms of the treaty, the exceptions to majority voting in the Council ceased to apply. In fact, fear of breaking up the Community has prevented use of this formal enlargement of power. That there were grounds for this fear was demonstrated by France's boycott of the Council's meetings from July 1965 to January 1966, over the issue of direct payment to the Community of customs duties levied on goods entering the Community from nonmember countries. This infraction of Article 5 of the Rome Treaty went unpenalized, for the Council still finds it prudent to bargain rather than attempt to dictate. The retention of the veto on the admission of new members (Art. 237) was graphically illustrated in December 1967 by France's repeated prevention of British membership. By making it a condition of her consent to the fusion of the executives of the three Communities under the treaty of 1965, France was also able to exclude Dr. Hallstein from the presidency of the combined Commission that came into office in 1967, thus eliminating a powerful advocate of political integration.

The complex diversity of tariffs, prices, wages, subsidies, labor conditions, and company law makes the fusion of the six states into one economic union a matter of constant and difficult political decision, and the European Communities have demonstrated the impossibility of isolating functional cooperation from the political preoccupations of the national governments. Five of the members have long held that the preservation of what has already been achieved, to say nothing of further economic and social progress, will call for closer political integration up to the point where a common European parliament and government would determine the course to be taken in the common interest. This would replace the present practice of negotiating compromises that tend to sacrifice that interest to narrowly conceived particular interests of the more powerful members. The five have ceased to rely, if they ever did rely, upon the doctrine that functional services will in due course bring about so general an identification of national and common interests that political division will painlessly fade away.

While political union might remove or reduce present obstacles to efficient operation, the European Communities have already worked prodigies of rationalization in a continent historically distinguished by bitter antagonisms. They have established a common liberty of migration and settlement and have made a rule of equal pay for men and women. They have unified most conditions and costs of transport. Uniform levels have been fixed for agricultural prices. Quotas on the exchange of goods between members were abolished as early as 1961. By July 1, 1968 intracommunity tariffs on both agricultural and industrial products had been abandoned and a common tariff fixed against outside countries. Methods of competition are now under collective control. The benefits reaped have made membership in the Economic Community or association with it a *desideratum* for many European and African countries.

Human Rights

The Rome Convention of 1950 with its subsequent protocols casts into treaty form much of the content of the United Nations' Universal Declaration of Human Rights.[11] It also establishes a European Commission of Human Rights and a Court of Human Rights. The power of the Commission to

---

[11] All members of the Council of Europe except France and Switzerland are parties to the Convention. Since October 6, 1962, Cyprus has been a party, and Malta ratified in January 1967.

hear petitions from private individuals depends upon optional acceptance of the relevant clause in the Convention, as does the jurisdiction of the Court. Eleven states (Austria, Belgium, Denmark, Federal Republic of Germany, Iceland, Ireland, Luxembourg, The Netherlands, Norway, Sweden, the United Kingdom) have granted the power to examine private petitions, and the Commission has dealt with large numbers of these, finding most of them too insubstantial to merit a hearing. In those that it has heard it has been able to effect an equitable adjustment. Individuals are not empowered to bring cases before the Court, but the Commission may refer doubtful decisions to it, and has done so in at least three cases. The eleven states listed above have accepted in advance the jurisdiction of the Court.

THE LEAGUE OF ARAB STATES

Because of their high degree of integration and the magnitude of their achievement, I have placed the European Communities ahead of a predecessor in time, the League of Arab States.

At the United Nations Conference on International Organization at San Francisco in 1945 (UNCIO), Egypt, Iraq, Lebanon, Saudi Arabia, and Syria were only less concerned than the Latin American countries to win full recognition for the principle of regional organization. Encouraged by the United Kingdom and the United States while the Second World War was still in progress, representatives of Egypt, Iraq, Lebanon, Syria, and Transjordan had joined in the Alexandria Protocol of October 7, 1944, announcing the intention to form a league of independent Arab states for mutual protection against aggression, for the pacific settlement of disputes, and for cooperation in economic, social, and cultural matters. This had been followed on March 22, 1945 by the Covenant of the League of Arab States, concluded by the heads of the same states plus those

137

of Saudi Arabia and the Yemen.[12] The latter instrument embodies the formal constitution of the League.

Thus, when they came to San Francisco in May 1945, the Arab delegates were seeking explicit recognition of a regional organization to which their countries were already committed. While they failed in this, as well as in the effort to incorporate in the Charter their own definition of regional organization, they did cooperate with the Latin American delegations to ensure that the Constitution of the United Nations gave its blessing to "regional arrangements or agencies for dealing with such matters relating to the maintenance of international peace and security as are appropriate for regional action, provided that such arrangements or agencies and their activities are consistent with the Purposes and Principles of the United Nations" (Art. 52.1).[13] There is no mention in the Charter of the regional activity in economic, social, and cultural matters which was the most prominent item in the Arab definition, but subsequent operations in these fields demonstrate the universal organization's policy of active cooperation with regional agencies.

Like the OAS, the Arab League has an elaborate structure of organs and agencies; but having seen how, after eighty years of operation, internecine strife still thwarts some of the best-laid plans of the former, we should not be surprised at the halting pace of the Arab organization.

One weakness, of course, lies in the unanimity rule for the governing Council and that body's lack of authority to enforce such decisions as it contrives to take. More serious are the stubborn underlying divergencies of national aims and policies. Iraq, which competes with the United Arab Re-

[12] The texts are translated in Muhammad Khalil, *The Arab States and the Arab League: A Documentary Record* (Beirut, 1962), 2: 53-61.

[13] UNCIO Documents, 11: 56-57; 12: 737, 833, 850, 857-858, 863-864.

public for leadership and has for considerable periods refused to attend Council meetings, brought the League close to dissolution in the period of its adherence to the Baghdad Pact and Central Treaty Organization. In 1950 Jordan was saved from expulsion over its annexation of Eastern Palestine only by a lack of unanimity in the Council. The endemic revolution in the Yemen divides the membership into royalist and republican factions. Conflicting territorial claims and complaints of intervention have from time to time brought fellow members into violent confrontation and led to requests for assistance from outside states or from the United Nations. The problems of economic integration are complicated by the clash of socialist and free-enterprise national systems, by wide differences in industrial development, and by the established European (especially French) direction of the commercial and financial relations of the four countries of the Maghreb. The Economic Committee provided for in the Covenant of 1945, the Economic Council established by the Joint Defense and Economic Cooperation Treaty of 1950, the Arab Development Bank, 1959-1964, the Council of Arab Economic Unity, 1964, and the Common Market agreed upon in the same year have thus far done little to justify the hopes that inspired their creation.[14] The most determined and effective economic action taken by the League continues to be the costly boycott of Israel directed by the Special Bureau at Damascus.

The Joint Defense and Economic Cooperation Treaty of 1950 pledged the parties to meet any threat of aggression by an immediate unification of plans, collective mobilization of resources, and the consolidation and coordination of their armed forces.[15] The war with Israel has revealed the

[14] See Alfred G. Musrey, *An Arab Common Market: A Study in Inter-Arab Trade Relations* (New York, 1969), esp. ch. 7; and Amin Dahbar, *Le Marché Commun Arabe et l'Oeuvre Economique de la Ligue Arabe* (Damascus, undated).

[15] Khalil, *loc.cit.*, pp. 101-105.

139

weaknesses of this alliance as a guarantee of regional security.

This disillusioning record is enough to explain a broad Western tendency to write the Arab League off as a negligible factor in world affairs. Such a judgment ignores positive accomplishments in the improvement of educational institutions and standards, in the preservation and enhancement of the common cultural heritage, in training for social service, in the interchange of medical knowledge, and in public health. It also ignores the League's success in unifying the positions taken by Arab delegations to international organizations, especially the United Nations, and securing the support of African delegations in issues such as the termination of colonialism, defense of national self-determination, and aid for development, where the nations of Africa and Asia are especially concerned. Through these delegations and its own observers, the League has had an important part in cementing the Afro-Asian bloc which, for better or worse, has become a dominant power in the General Assembly.[16]

The League of Arab States also plays a significant role in the development and codification of international law. This it does through its members' delegates and its own observers in the competent bodies of the United Nations, working here again in partnership with the African states. A special body for this collaboration was established in 1956 by Burma, Ceylon, India, Indonesia, Iraq, Japan, and Syria. This is the Asian-African Legal Consultative Committee which has since added the UAR, Pakistan, Morocco, Ghana, the Sudan, and Thailand to its membership. Constant pressure is maintained by this Committee to secure wider representation of the Asian and African countries in the various

---

[16] A much-needed corrective to the excessively negative Western estimate has been provided by Robert W. Macdonald in *The League of Arab States* (Princeton, 1965).

organs and agencies of the United Nations, and full consideration of the positions taken by them in the adaptation of the international legal order to the contemporary world. Its annual sessions, attended by observers from the Arab League, the International Law Commission of the United Nations, and the United Nations Secretariat, discuss the subjects being prepared by the ILC for codification. This work is systematized by a permanent secretariat situated in New Delhi, and its results are communicated to the ILC, to which the Committee sends observers. There is also an exchange of observers with the Organization of American States, the Organization of African Unity, and the International Institute for the Unification of Private Law.[17]

THE ORGANIZATION OF AFRICAN UNITY

This regional organization was set up by a Conference of African States assembled at Cairo in May 1963. The original membership numbered thirty-two, and eight more states had been added by 1968. The Charter, after a Preamble affirming the adherence of the parties to the principles of the United Nations Charter and the Universal Declaration of Human Rights, dedicates the OAU to the eradication of all forms of colonialism from Africa, to self-determination and equality for all peoples, and to cooperation in defense and in political, economic, and social development.

The structural debt of the Organization to the European Communities is obvious. An Assembly of Heads of State and Government, whose resolutions on substantive matters re-

[17] For the organization and activities of the Committee, see the Reports of its sessions issued by the Secretariat in New Delhi. Professor R. P. Anand of the Indian School of International Studies has emphasized the importance, in the evolution of a supranational legal order, of the reconciliation of Eastern and Western conceptions, to which the Consultative Committee is dedicated. See esp. his articles in AJIL, 56 (1962), 383-406, and ICLQ, 15 (1966), pt. 1, 55-75. Compare M. K. Nawaz in ASIL *Proceedings*, 1963, pp. 275-293.

quire a two-thirds majority, meets at least once a year. Acting under its instructions and implementing its decisions is a Council of Ministers which acts by simple majority. The Charter provides for five Specialized Commissions—Economic and Social; Educational and Cultural; Health, Sanitation and Nutrition; Defense; Scientific, Technical and Research.[18]

One significant difference from the European model is the lack of any power of enforcement. Another is the absence of a court of justice. The peaceful settlement to which the members are pledged is to be sought by "negotiation, mediation, conciliation or arbitration." This suggests, and subsequent experience has demonstrated, a distinct preference for the less formal modes of dealing with the multifarious conflicts that were bound to develop among forty ill-defined but determinedly sovereign fragments of the former colonial empires.

The supreme object of the OAU thus far has been the elimination of colonial domination and racial discrimination from every part of Africa. This has been the driving force in the prolonged but unavailing efforts of the United Nations to expel Portugal from Africa, to terminate the South African Republic's control of Namibia, to reverse the policy of apartheid, to induce the United Kingdom to use any force needed to overthrow the racist government of Rhodesia, and to unite the membership in sanctions designed to enforce the long series of resolutions to these ends.

[18] The Charter, and *Proceedings* up to February, 1964, are to be found in *Organization of African Unity, Basic Documents and Resolutions*, issued by the Provisional Secretariat.

See B. Boutros-Ghali, *L'Organization de l'Unité Africaine* (Paris, 1969), for an admirably detached and scholarly analysis of plans and performance. The system of Specialist Committees, this author points out, has never worked well, and conflicting proposals to expand or contract it have impeded the substantive work of the OAU. See esp. pp. 130-133, 170.

The absorbing aim of winning Africa for the Africans has been pursued by the OAU at the expense of its economic, social, and cultural plans. Even so, it is far from achievement. The fanatical nationalism of a bevy of states in the first flush of independence defies effective unification of policy and submission to overall leadership. Poverty of resources, perpetuated by unwillingness to concentrate upon economic development, cripples the Organization's campaign to liberate the continent. The continuing strategic and economic interests of the greater Powers, source of that "neo-colonialism" which OAU leaders denounce no less stridently than the formal remnants of European imperialism, temper the energy of the United Nations' response to African complaints.

Seven years are little time for any international association to prove itself, and the task of integration in Africa is at least as formidable as in any other region. Yet the record is by no means totally negative. It shows a modicum of success that warrants hope.

Let us take, for example, the field of pacific settlement. On the negative side we must note that the Commission of Mediation, Conciliation and Arbitration, provided for by Article XIX of the Charter, was not set up and manned until 1965, and up to 1968 had not been used. On the other hand, *ad hoc* methods adopted by the Heads of State and Government or the Council of Ministers, while they failed to mitigate the horrors of the Nigerian revolution, have in several instances mediated disputes that had erupted or threatened to erupt into violence. In this field, as in others, the United Nations has been at pains to use, and so to strengthen, the Organization in its regional activity. Thus, on December 30, 1964, the Security Council adopted Resolution 199 (Doc. S/6129) endorsing the OAU's efforts to assist the Government of the Democratic Republic of the Congo along the road of national reconciliation, requesting all states to sup-

143

port these efforts, and asking to be kept informed. As late as September 1968, U Thant advised that the best channel for external pressure toward a just peace in Nigeria lay through the Organization.[19]

Among Africa's most urgent problems is the resettlement of the thousands of refugees uprooted by widespread civil strife. Here the United Nations High Commissioner for Refugees relies increasingly upon the OAU and has expressed his appreciation of the liberal measures taken by member states.[20]

The practice of mutual reinforcement is beginning to produce results even in the field of economic development, where the expert and experienced staff of the United Nations Economic Commission for Africa (ECA) has placed its services at the disposal of the OAU in what is essentially a common task. This not only helps the regional organization in its approach to the complex problems of modernization; it wins good will for the ECA in the performance of its mandate from the UN.[21] But perhaps the most important example of mutual reinforcement lies in yet another domain, namely disarmament. At various times the governing bodies of OAU have declared their interest in general disarmament with special emphasis upon the nonproliferation of nuclear weapons. Their series of proposals on the subject came to a head in a Declaration adopted at Cairo in July 1964 and endorsed on October 10, 1964 by the Conference of Non-Aligned Countries in the same city. The essence of this pronouncement was the urgent appeal to all states to recognize the African continent as a denuclearized zone. This was taken up and approved by the General Assembly

[19] *United Nations Monthly Chronicle*, October 1969, p. 56.

[20] See the High Commissioner's Annual Reports, 1964-1968, and General Assembly Resolution 2040 (xx).

[21] For surveys of UN-OAU cooperation, see the Secretary-General's Reports, GAOR, A/6174 (December 16, 1965), and GAOR, A/6885 (November 1, 1967).

of the United Nations on December 3, 1965 in Resolution 2033 (xx), which repeated the injunction upon all states to refrain from testing, manufacturing, using, threatening to use, or deploying nuclear weapons in Africa.[22]

REGIONAL ORGANIZATIONS AND THE UNITED NATIONS

We have seen how various organs of the United Nations cooperate with regional agencies in programs of economic development, attempt to reinforce approved regional efforts to keep the peace, and take counsel with their spokesmen on problems encountered in the development and codification of international law. We have also seen how members of regional organizations may appeal to the United Nations to curb alleged aggressions or interventions by fellow members. All of this was to be expected, given the statutory duty and authority of the universal organization to promote the modernization of economic and social institutions and to deal with threats to the peace wherever they occur. It was also to be expected, especially in the exercise of peace-keeping functions, that disputes would occur about the division of competence between the two levels of organization. These have been particularly sharp in the relations between the Organization of American States and the United Nations. There they have been a minor incident in the cold war with the United States on the one side counting upon its ability to make its policies prevail in the regional organization and averse to interference from the United Nations, where its early predominance had foundered in the influx of new members; and the Soviet Union on the other, seeking to spread its influence in Latin America and to use the United Nations as a counter to Washington's power there.

The pattern was already set in the 1954 proceedings of

[22] Text in UNYB, 1965, p. 81. See also GAOR, A/5975 (September 23, 1965), and A/6127 (December 2, 1965).

the Security Council in connection with Guatemala's complaint of aid given by Honduras and Nicaragua to Colonel Castillo Armas in his revolt against the Arbenz regime. There a resolution sponsored by Brazil and Colombia to refer the complaint to the OAS was heartily supported by the United States, which had also afforded assistance to Castillo,[23] but vetoed by the sole dissenting vote cast by the USSR. In this instance, however, a compromise proposed by France was adopted unanimously in a resolution requesting the Council, without prejudice to any measures taken by the OAS, to call for immediate cessation of action likely to cause further bloodshed and to bid all members of the United Nations to abstain from assisting such action. The spokesman for the United States had argued a duty to exhaust the regional possibilities of settlement before referring a dispute to the United Nations. Ambiguities arising out of the wording of Articles 33-35 and Article 52.4 of the Charter lend support to the opposing argument of concurrent jurisdiction. In the absence of any authoritative decision of this debate, it is easy to argue legally for a position taken for essentially political reasons.[24]

In the critical confrontation of the two Super powers in October 1962, President Kennedy announced on the evening of the twenty-second (a) that a quarantine was being initiated on offensive military equipment shipped to Cuba; (b) that an immediate meeting of the Organ of Consultation of OAS was being called for; and (c) that an emergency meeting of the UN Security Council was being requested "to take action against this latest Soviet threat to world peace."

The quarantine had thus been decided upon before consultation either with the OAS or with the UN; but, as announced in the President's Proclamation of October 23, was

[23] See Dwight D. Eisenhower, *Mandate For Change* (New York, 1963), pp. 424-427.

[24] SCOR, 9th Year, 675th and 676th meetings.

not to operate until 2 p.m. on October 24. In the interval, the oas had by a vote of nineteen to nought adopted its Resolution recommending that "the member states . . . take all measures, individually and collectively, which they may deem necessary to ensure that the government of Cuba cannot continue to receive from the Sino-Soviet Powers military material and related supplies which may threaten the peace and security of the continent and to prevent the missiles in Cuba with offensive capability from ever becoming an active threat to the peace and security of the continent." This unanimous mandate from the regional organization could not have been more absolute.[25]

No such authority was granted by the United Nations. Between the twenty-third and twenty-fifth of October, the Security Council had before it (a) a resolution proposed by the United States and calling "as a provisional measure under Article 40 for the immediate dismantling and withdrawal from Cuba of all missiles and other offensive weapons"; (b) a request from Cuba "to consider the act of war unilaterally committed by the Government of the United States in ordering the naval blockade of Cuba . . . in absolute contempt of the Security Council"; (c) a draft resolution from the ussr condemning the us for violating the Charter and increasing the threat of war, and calling upon the us to lift its blockade and negotiate with the ussr and Cuba to remove the threat; and (d) a draft resolution sponsored by Ghana and the United Arab Republic requesting that the Acting Secretary-General confer with the parties to remove the existing threat to world peace, and calling upon the parties to assist him in this task and to refrain from further aggravation of the situation.

None of these motions reached a vote. On October 25, the Council suspended discussion pending negotiations which, on U Thant's direct appeal, the us and ussr had agreed to

[25] dsb, November 12, 1962, pp. 715-720, 722, 724, 740-746.

undertake. After a visit to Havana, October 30-31, U Thant was able to report progress in the dismantling of the missiles and agreement of the parties "that the UN should continue to participate in the peaceful settlement of the problem."

The sequel is too well known to require retelling here. It is worthwhile, however, to recall that the Soviet Union and the United States joined in a letter dated January 7, 1963,[26] thanking the Secretary-General for his assistance in preserving the peace. Cuba was less grateful. The letter addressed by the Cuban Government to U Thant on the same day was to the effect that the Secretary-General's mediation had not "led to an effective agreement capable of guaranteeing in a permanent way the peace of the Caribbean."[27] This disparaging note did not affect the general conviction that the United Nations had played a decidedly useful role in the most alarming crisis of the postwar years.

There remains the question of the conformity of the action taken by the United States with the Charter of the United Nations. That the Legal Division of the Department of State was far from content with the view expressed by Mr. Acheson that international law had no bearing on the conduct of a state faced with so grave a peril is evident from the position taken by the Legal Adviser, Mr. Abram Chayes. In the same proceedings where the former Secretary of State made his pronouncement, and again in his article in the April 1963 number of *Foreign Affairs*, Mr. Chayes made clear his deep concern with the legal aspects of the Cuban crisis. The quarantine was in his view neither action under Article 51 nor force ordered by the United Nations, but fell within a third category, that of "action by regional organizations to preserve the peace." As the Council of the OAS had done in its Resolution of October 23, he

[26] DSB, January 28, 1963, p. 153.
[27] UNYB, 1962, p. 111.

cites the Inter-American Treaty of Reciprocal Assistance of 1947 (the Rio Treaty). Article 6 of that instrument calls for an immediate meeting "if the inviolability or the integrity of the territory or political independence of any American state should be affected by an aggression which is not an armed attack or by any other fact or situation that might endanger the peace of America . . . in order to agree on the measures which should be taken for the common defense and for the maintenance of the peace and security of the continent." Article 8 lists the measures that may be agreed upon, and these include the use of armed force.

General international law does not prohibit the supply of arms by one state to another. Under that law, the installation of missiles in Cuba was no more illegal than that along the Black Sea coast of Turkey. Was it a threat to the peace of America? If so, it would come within the competence of the UN and, subject to a condition shortly to be mentioned, of the OAS. On this question, the grave view taken in Washington, and the rare unanimity of OAS support, are persuasive. There is an inevitable psychological, subjective element in the perception of threat. Here, the century-old Monroe Doctrine, warning intruders off the hemisphere, was being defied.

But, under Article 6 of the Rio Treaty, danger to the peace is not enough. The act constituting the danger must affect "the inviolability or the integrity of the territory or the sovereignty or political independence" of the target state. Since the installation of the missiles was proceeding with the willing consent of the Cuban government, was this condition satisfied? The answer, so far as official American opinion is concerned, is to be found in the 1954 Declaration of Caracas, which records "the determination of the American states to take the necessary measures to protect their political independence against the intervention of international communism acting in the interest of an alien despo-

149

tism." Cuba, under another government, was a party to this Declaration.

In the ASIL *Proceedings* of 1963 already cited, Professor Quincy Wright suggested that Security Council authorization may not have been necessary because the OAS Resolution was a mere recommendation to members and therefore not enforcement action by the Organization itself. I would contend that a recommendation acted upon by the United States as a request and authorization to use armed force was enforcement action by a regional agency and required therefore the authorization stipulated in Article 53. After all, the Organization is precluded by Article 20 of the Rio Treaty from *ordering* any member to use armed force, and this can hardly mean that this mode of enforcement, undertaken in the name of the Organization, is never to be classified as its own action.

Mr. Chayes apparently takes this position, since he is at pains to persuade us that, as interpreted in Security Council proceedings in regard to sanctions imposed by the OAS upon the Dominican Republic in 1960, authorization does not necessarily mean prior approval, and that the requirement may be met by a mere taking note of regional enforcement measures. In the instant case the Legal Adviser was apparently satisfied by the Security Council's failure to adopt either of the condemnatory resolutions submitted. This reduces authorization to mere information.

Mr. Chayes was arguing for a reasonable interpretation, in 1962, of a text which, in 1945, prescribed the relationship between regional arrangements and the United Nations in the matter of enforcement. It was obvious that the Soviet Union would veto Security Council approval of naval action to prevent arms from reaching Cuba and that the United States must either establish its "quarantine" without prior authorization or not at all. It did at once inform the Security Council of what it was planning to do, and submitted a

150

draft resolution calling for the dismantling and withdrawal of the missiles. This marked a formal deference to the Charter. I find it difficult to believe that any impartial tribunal, bearing in mind that the peace-keeping machinery planned in 1945 had been left far from complete, and that any practical action within the Security Council's power was certain to be vetoed, could find the United States guilty of a violation of existing law in acting as it had. The decision would, I believe, be the same if the United States had relied on Article 51.[28] The tribunal might perhaps note in an *obiter dictum* that whereas Washington had consistently refused to admit that anything but a wartime blockade could legally stop shipping other than that of the blockaded state, it was now instituting, under the mollifying title "quarantine," action which differed only in its limitation to weapons and military equipment from the pacific blockade practiced in the nineteenth century by other maritime powers.

The record leaves no doubt that the Security Council has been unable to exercise anything approaching the control over regional organizations that the Charter prescribed.[29] This should not overshadow the fact that in the Cuban crisis and again in the sequel to the 1964 intervention of the United States in the Dominican Republic the United Nations was able to contribute substantially to peaceful settlement. In reference to the Dominican conflict of 1964-1965, the Secretary-General notes that this was "the first time a United Nations Mission had operated in the same area and dealt with the same matters as an operation of a regional association" and that the mission "had played a major part in bringing about a cessation of hostilities."[30] What has happened in the relationship with regional agencies is a work-

[28] See above, p. 148.

[29] Cf. Inis Claude, in *International Conciliation*, no. 547, March 1964.

[30] UNYB, 1965, p. 155.

ing adaptation of constitutional prescriptions to circumstances not anticipated when the text was drawn up. The United Nations has had to content itself with the role of diplomatic coordination rather than legal control.

6.

LAW AND WAR TODAY

WE have seen[1] how, in the early formulation of the
law of nations, war was the center of attention, the norms
for peaceful relations being primarily a statement of the
rights and duties nonobservance of which justified recourse
to war. In the same context we saw how, even up to 1914,
the great "lawmaking" conferences, including the "Peace
Conferences" of 1899 and 1907, were predominantly concerned with clarifying and augmenting the laws of war and
neutrality. The war of 1914-1918, we observed, brought in
its train a change of emphasis, the great object thenceforth
being, not the mitigation of the horrors of war, but a legal
system replacing war as a mode of settling international
disputes.

The achievement of such a system has proved far more
difficult than the draftsmen of 1919 or 1945 appear to have
anticipated. At any rate, the structure they built was in both
cases far from adequate to the task of keeping the peace. Its
inadequacies and failures, marked by successive outbreaks
of large-scale violence, lend some cogency to the argument
that the adaptation of the laws of war to contemporary
modes of combat merits serious effort. As the reader will
discover, I nevertheless do not find this thesis generally
persuasive, and lean rather to prevention than to palliation.

My reasons are as follows. Considering, first, nuclear war,
it is scarcely plausible that any state will obey Article I of
Hague Convention III (1907) by either a summary declara-

---

[1] Above, pp. 34-37.

tion or a conditional ultimatum before launching a nuclear attack, even where the immediate threat is a limited tactical use of the new weapons. To do so would be to invite a first strike. Recent practice indeed suggests that even for conventional war Article 1 has become a dead letter. However that may be, the existing rules on the conduct of hostilities and on relations between belligerents and neutrals would be largely inapplicable to the swift and appalling course of nuclear war once launched. If enough is left on either side to call for military occupation, there might be some purpose in invoking the Hague Rules. But the whole prospect is so incalculable that no effort is being made to draft rules for nuclear war and a good deal is being devoted to preventing its outbreak. Prohibition of the production and use of nuclear weapons is the announced aim of official disarmament projects, while, as interim restraints, a nonproliferation treaty is sponsored by the United States, the Soviet Union, and the United Kingdom, and a "no-first-use" rule is being urged upon all possessors of nuclear armaments.

Insofar as "conventional" war may be carried on between established states by regular forces operating under clear chains of command, there is still doubtless a place for the laws of war. Those already on the books are largely sufficient, and the problem is to secure their observance. They are being invoked with little success in Vietnam, where "conventional" mingles with guerrilla warfare.

Guerrilla warfare seems by its very nature to defy regulation. Though it may follow prearranged general patterns, the units involved act largely on their own initiative as occasion offers, use any means at hand, and dissolve indistinguishably at need into the ordinary population.

The wars that continue to wreak havoc in a world no less prone to violence than in the darkest periods of its history do not take the form of open and direct violence between rival states. They have their origin in civil war fomented

154

and exploited by foreign governments as a mode of preserving or expanding national power, and they lend themselves generously to guerrilla tactics. Their tendency to expand into large-scale international conflict is illustrated by Korea (1950-1953) and Vietnam (1954-). They are not announced by any declaration or ultimatum; there is no place for the customary laws of neutrality; and even the relevance of the Geneva Conventions of 1949 on prisoners of war and civilian populations, in spite of express provisions for their application in civil war, is disputed by reservations and captious interpretations. The fragmentary and controversial rules relating to belligerency and insurgency, as they evolved in the American Civil War of 1861-1865 and the Spanish Civil War of 1936-1938, have proved woefully irrelevant, and we are faced with a multitude of grave problems for which there is not even an agreed academic solution, to say nothing of an officially accepted code. Where, as in Latin America, theoretically binding conventions prohibit intervention and the fomenting or supporting of civil strife, these have been systematically ignored; while action in the United Nations has been prevented by ideological and strategic rivalries of the Great Powers. The cases involving Latin American countries have been further complicated by competition between regional and United Nations jurisdiction, in which the former, actively championed by the United States, has usually won.

Foreign intervention in civil strife is far from new. One has only to think of the Holy Alliance to realize that this has long been a mode of propagating an ideology (in that instance monarchical legitimacy versus revolutionary liberalism), or of serving other national interests, by preventing the defeat or assisting the return to power of a friendly government. What is new is the extent to which this form of conflict has displaced open war in the power struggle that still wastes the resources of nations large and small.

Can we at least formulate a body of consistent rules which, if enforced, would eliminate this type of war? Rationally interpreted and applied, the United Nations Charter, with its principle of self-determination and its prohibitions of force, would already serve this vital purpose. But apart from ambiguities that provide specious pleas for unilateral resort to force as an instrument of aggressive policy, there is a lack in that text of specific reference to foreign participation in internal conflict. This has become far too perilous to be left without explicit regulation.

Let us begin with the question whether foreign assistance rendered at the request of a recognized government to suppress revolt is or should be permissible. There was some debate on this subject even in the positivist nineteenth century, though it might have been thought difficult for writers who found the law in the customary practice of states to support the negative. W. E. Hall, for example, disputed the legality of unilateral intervention in favor of either side and regardless of request, but was prepared to concede "a wider range of intervention" to the "body of states."[2] Since the Charter of the United Nations came into force, this has become a common thesis. Yet in the last twenty years the Soviet Union, the United States, and the United Kingdom have all sent armed forces to assist a favored group in establishing or maintaining itself as government of a foreign country. This was the case in Hungary, the Lebanon, Jordan, Vietnam, the Dominican Republic, and Czechoslovakia. Even the United Nations has failed thus far to take a firm stand against states aiding an established government. Louis Sohn reminds us that the Security Council in 1946 rejected Soviet proposals to condemn Great Britain for affording military aid to the governments of Greece and of Indonesia.[3]

[2] A *Treatise on International Law*, 3rd ed. (Oxford, 1890), pp. 290-91.
[3] "The Role of the United Nations in Civil War," in *The Strategy*

As justification for the action taken, intervening powers commonly cite subversive intervention or military aid to rebels already initiated by another, and plead collective self-defense against alleged invasion. The assisted government has in some cases been one whose support came less from any expressed will of its nationals than from the intervening power; and its request for assistance has been invited by that power.

As for assistance to rebels, the Soviet Union and its allies still insist upon the legality of assisting "wars of liberation," that is to say any revolutions aiming at the overthrow of regimes of which they disapprove. That an essentially identical rationale may be adopted by a Western power is indicated by the Bay of Pigs incident of 1961.

A concise review of events in Vietnam since the Second World War will serve to show how little in the way of established guidelines the existing international order provides for the conduct of foreign governments in the kind of struggle that has brought twenty-five years of slaughter and destruction to the Vietnamese, and what a mockery can be made of such frail restraints as either the general law of nations or the United Nations Charter has tried to impose. If good can come of this long agony, the best could be a general conviction that intervention in civil strife must no longer be left to the discretion of governments, however lofty their declared intentions.

The undeclared war in Vietnam began as a struggle, under the leadership of Ho Chi Minh and his League for Vietnam Independence (Vietminh), to free Tonkin, Annam, and Cochin-China from all foreign domination. By 1945 the Vietminh had gathered strength enough to take over the government of Tonkin as the Japanese withdrew, to proclaim the sovereignty of the Democratic Republic of Vietnam (DRV), and even to assume power in Annam and

of World Order, ed. Richard A. Falk and Saul H. Mendlovitz, 4 vols. (New York, 1966), 3: 584.

Cochin-China. Unification was halted by the Potsdam arrangements for restoring the country to France. The French reentry was assisted in the South by the occupying forces of Great Britain and in the North by those of the Kuomintang. In 1946, the Vietminh and the People's Army of Vietnam (PAV) launched the drive which in 1954 ended with the annihilating defeat of the French at Dien Bien Phu.

By 1950 the United States, which in 1945 had assisted the Vietminh in its guerrilla operations against the Japanese, had come to regard that organization as a spearhead of Communism. Recognition of the DRV by the Soviet Union and by the freshly victorious People's Republic of China was, for Washington, confirmation of this assessment. By way of building up resistance to what it envisaged as a drive for Chinese control of the peninsula, the Truman Administration in February 1950 joined the United Kingdom in recognizing the ex-emperor Bao Dai, France's choice, as head of a State of Vietnam, which purported to unite Cochin-China, Annam, and Tonkin as one of the Associated States of Indo-China and a member of the French Union. Secretary of State Acheson sounded the familiar anti-Communist refrain, announcing the grant of economic aid and military equipment to the Associated States and to France to help preserve the national independence and democratic evolution which could not "exist in any area dominated by Soviet imperialism."[4]

American involvement had begun. Military and political advisers were provided, and financial aid soon rose to more than half a billion dollars a year. Even so, the combined forces of France and Bao Dai's State of Vietnam could not stem the victorious progress of the Vietminh and its PAV. By March 1954, Secretary of State Dulles was calling for allied action to prevent "the impression on Southeast Asia of the political system of Communist Russia and its Chinese Com-

[4] DSB, May 22, 1950, p. 821.

munist ally" which, he said, "must be a grave threat to the whole free community."[5] His appeal was rejected by Great Britain, and the ensuing Geneva Conference offered him little consolation. The concession there made to the DRV seemed to him an excessive and dangerous price to pay for a cessation of hostilities that momentarily saved French face. By way of shoring up the weakened anti-Communist front in the area, he organized the conference which at Manila in September 1954 concluded the Southeast Asia Collective Defense Treaty (SACDT) with its Protocol covering Cambodia, Laos, "and the free territory under the jurisdiction of the State of Vietnam."

SACDT had the attraction for most of its signatories that it contained no firm pledge of military action—a fact ignored by those who justify United States military intervention in Vietnam as something to which the country is explicitly bound by that instrument. What each party agreed to do in the eventualities specified was to "consult immediately" and to "act to meet the common danger in accordance with its constitutional processes." De Gaulle's France took advantage of this vagueness to ignore resolutions of the Council set up by the treaty and of the Manila Conference of 1966, calling for continued military and economic assistance until the Communists had desisted from their aggression against South Vietnam.

The Geneva Conference resulted in agreements ending hostilities between the forces of the DRV and those of the French Union in Cambodia, Laos, and Vietnam. An International Commission for Supervision and Control (ICSC), composed of representatives of Canada, India, and Poland, was set up for each of the three countries. The sole parties to these agreements, strictly speaking, were France and the DRV, acting through their high commands in Indo-China. In a Final Declaration, however, all members of the Confer-

[5] DSB, April 12, 1954, pp. 539-40.

ence except the United States and the State of Vietnam (that is to say, the Soviet Union, the Chinese People's Republic, the United Kingdom, France, the Democratic Republic of Vietnam, Cambodia, and Laos) took note of the agreements, emphasized their interpretation of the terms, and undertook to consult on questions referred by the ICSC and to study measures to secure observance of the agreements on the cessation of hostilities in Cambodia, Laos, and Vietnam.

In what follows, "the Agreement" means the one laying down details for the cease-fire in Vietnam, which was by far the most immediately important. This provided for withdrawal of the opposing forces into the zones north and south respectively of a provisional military demarcation line drawn along the seventeenth parallel of North Latitude and a demilitarized zone extending to five kilometers on each side of the demarcation line. In both north and south withdrawal zones the agreement prohibited reinforcement of troops and war material and adherence to any military alliance.

In the closing session of the Conference, Bedell Smith, as US Representative, said that his government was "not prepared to join in a Declaration by the Conference such as is submitted," but would make a unilateral declaration. This took note of all the agreements reached and of all the paragraphs of the Final Declaration except the last, which contains the undertaking to consult and to study measures. The unilateral declaration went on to say that the United States Government "will refrain from the threat or the use of force to disturb" the agreements and paragraphs and "would view any renewal of aggression in violation of the aforesaid agreements with grave concern and as seriously threatening international peace and security."

The representatives of the State of Vietnam had been excluded from the formal negotiations of the Conference in

160

deference to the insistence of the DRV that it alone must speak for all Vietnam. In its final session the Conference took note of a declaration by the Saigon Government to the effect that it undertook "to make and support every effort to re-establish a real and lasting peace in Vietnam" and "not to use force to resist the procedures for carrying the cease-fire into effect, in spite of the objections and reservations that the State of Vietnam has expressed." The objections were directed to provisions threatening the unity and independence of Vietnam, especially to any division of its territory, however provisional and temporary, and to the holding of elections before the Security Council was satisfied that conditions for a free vote had been established. Bao Dai's delegates had also demanded that in any settlement reached, the State of Vietnam should be recognized as the sole legal authority for the country as a whole. If these points were settled in its favor, Saigon declared itself willing to accept the result of a general election held under the supervision of the United Nations. The Final Declaration of the Conference stipulated that the elections should be held in July 1956, and that representatives of the two zones should begin consultations on appropriate arrangements on July 20, 1955. Supervision was to be in the hands of representatives of the three states composing the ICSC. These provisions the Saigon Government consistently refused to accept, just as it stubbornly denied the validity of the demarcation line.

Early in July 1954 Bao Dai had appointed Ngo Dinh Diem prime minister of the State of Vietnam. This eminent Vietnamese Catholic was in great favor in the United States, where he had spent several years and made himself *persona gratissima* with the Roman Catholic hierarchy. To him President Eisenhower wrote on October 23, 1954, expressing concern over the implications of the Geneva Agreement for "a country temporarily divided by an arti-

161

ficial military grouping, weakened by a long and exhausting war, and faced with enemies without and by their sub-versive collaborators within," and offering increased aid, "provided that your Government is prepared to give assur-ance as to the standards of performance it would be able to maintain in the event such aid were supplied."[6] Exactly a year later a plebiscite in South Vietnam decided that Diem should replace Bao Dai as head of state, and on October 26, 1955 Diem proclaimed the Republic of Vietnam with him-self as president.

In April 1956 France, weakened by the long and costly struggle with the DRV and now battling revolt in Algeria, withdrew from Vietnam. The fulfillment of the Geneva Agreement, her responsibility south of the demarcation line, was thus left dependent upon the good will of the Saigon Government which, as we have seen, was not a party, de-nied any succession to France's obligation, and continued to protest a settlement reached over its objections. In this negative position it was supported by the United States which, exultantly satisfied with Diem's "standards of per-formance," granted increasing aid. In some important re-spects the record from 1955 to 1960 was indeed com-mendable. Good use was made of strong US assistance in resettling almost a million refugees from the North, most of them Roman Catholic. The armed religious sects battling what they regarded, not without reason, as a systematic at-tempt to fasten a Roman Catholic monopoly of power upon a people three-quarters Buddhist, were brought tempo-rarily under control; and substantial reforms were effected in a criminally corrupt police system. A general program of social and economic development was hailed in the United States as a triumph for democratic foreign aid.

Unhappily the people was far from united behind its president. In 1958-1959 guerrilla operations by Communists

[6] DSB, November 15, 1954, pp. 735-36.

and nationalists associated in the Vietcong, and assisted by Hanoi, disrupted life in the villages; while the harsh countermeasures adopted by the police under Diem's brother Ngo Dinh Nhu, and the anti-Buddhist maneuvers of Mme. Nhu, alienated support from the ruling family. An army coup against them in 1960 failed; but in spite of Diem's large majority in the 1961 presidential election, the breakdown of order in the face of widespread Vietcong successes reached a critical stage. In this emergency President Kennedy ordered a large increase in both economic and military aid. The latter category now included, in addition to advisers and technicians, propeller-driven fighter aircraft with pilots and mechanics.[7] Military personnel rose from one thousand to twelve thousand in 1961-1962. After a second military coup had assassinated Diem and Nhu in 1963, a rapid succession of governments attested the confusion and corruption of the political-military-fabric; but American aid went on rising in a feverish effort to impose stability on a quicksand. In February 1965 American aircraft began bombing the North, and within four months American combat forces were engaged in land, sea, and air operations against the Vietcong in South Vietnam. By 1968 these forces numbered more than a half a million. Operating with them were the larger South Vietnamese army and minor contingents from Australia, New Zealand, the Philippines, South Korea, and Thailand. The incessant and wide-ranging battle between these allied forces and the powerful and elusive guerrillas, reinforced by regular troops from the DRV, has brought devastation to the land, destruction to its cities and, in addition to mounting military casualties, death to thousands of its civilian population. It is hardly conceivable that a take-over by Hanoi, with its probable sequel of murderous purges, could have led to anything approaching the tragedy that has followed upon what was undoubtedly a

[7] Roger Hilsman, *To Move a Nation* (New York, 1967), pp. 416-18.

sincere desire to defeat Communism and promote democracy. One task for a new law of nations will be to control the misguided benevolence of states.

Inevitably the opposing sides accuse each other of violating the general law of nations, the United Nations Charter, and the Geneva Agreement of 1954. Charges of aggression, that crime that the United Nations cannot define, hurtle back and forth. The Soviet bloc joins the DRV and the Chinese People's Republic in this polemic, and their official position is faithfully echoed in Communist legal symposia and periodicals. An occasional article in the legal literature of countries not directly involved has a more analytical and judicial tone.[8] But the most lively argument goes on in the United States, where an important part of the legal fraternity disputes the legality and the morality of what Washington is doing in Vietnam. American religious organizations are to be found on both sides of the debate, and their opposing positions are fortified by elaborate legal briefs. Washington publishes official defenses bolstered by lists of illegalities on the part of the DRV and its allies. These are quoted with approval, or rebutted, by supporters or assailants of the government's policy. The interchange is doing much to instruct an intelligent public in the law of nations at its present stage and to reveal its need of clarification and development.[9]

[8] See for example, J. A. Frowein, "Völkerrechtliche Aspekte des Vietnam-Konfliktes," in *Zeitschrift fur Ausländisches Öffentliches Recht und Völkerrecht*, July 1967, pp. 1-23; and Henri Meyrowitz, "Le Droit de la Guerre dans le Conflit Vietnamien," in *Annuaire Français de Droit International Public*, 1967, pp. 153-201.

[9] American arguments for and against the legality and morality of the action of the United States in Vietnam are collected in *The Vietnam War and International Law*, ed. Richard A. Falk (Princeton, 1968). See also, the Consultative Council of the Lawyers' Committee on American Policy Towards Vietnam, *Vietnam and International Law* (Flanders, N.J., 1967); United Presbyterian Church in the USA, *Vietnam, The Christian, the Gospel, the Church* (Philadelphia, 1967);

The extent to which the United States and Saigon were bound by the Geneva Agreements of 1954 is still debated. The International Commission for Supervision and Control has however found repeated violations of the cease-fire provisions on both sides of the demarcation line, and it is plain that both the Agreements and the 1962 Declaration on the Neutralization of Laos have been systematically disregarded by the contending forces. Military operations in the demilitarized zone are of common occurrence, while Hanoi's use of Laotian territory for infiltration and supply routes to South Vietnam, and allied attacks upon these routes, are a matter of common knowledge.

Relatively successful in its initial conciliatory efforts following the cease-fire, the ICSC, which was never given any powers of enforcement, has since been unable either to supervise or to control. Its frail formal authority was overwhelmed in an escalation that has transformed what was originally an anti-colonial revolution in one comparatively small country into a violent phase of the world's current power struggle.

The same transformation explains the inability of the United Nations to deal with a breakdown of the international order which that Organization was designed to establish and maintain. When, in Feburary 1966, the United States succeeded in having Vietnam placed on the agenda of the Security Council, the struggle in Southeast Asia had become complicated by bitterly opposed Great-Power interests and had taken on dimensions that paralyzed the weak machinery of peace. The president of the Security Council, after soundings among the membership, reported "a general feeling that it would be inopportune for the Council to hold further debate at this time." In the same context he pointed out that the matter remained on the

Clergy and Laymen Concerned about Vietnam, *In the Name of America* (New York, 1968).

Council's agenda. That being so, only a request from the Council would enable the General Assembly, which discusses the conflict at length in its annual sessions, to make any recommendation upon it in accordance with Charter Article 12.[10] Clearly, if the United Nations is to deal effectively with internal conflicts serious enough to threaten international peace, it must be seized of them at an early stage in their development.

It may be argued that the Charter, supplemented by such anti-intervention resolutions as 2131 (xx) and 2225 (xxi), adopted by the General Assembly in 1965 and 1966, already provides sufficient legal ground for any collective action that is at present politically possible. It cannot be denied that the essential and most difficult problem here, as at so many points in the international order, is one not of formulation but of enforcement. If so, why waste energy adding to the existing volume of unenforced norms?

There are at least two answers to this question. One is the demonstrated need for agreed rules, precisely defined, to meet problems that have taken on new urgency. In some areas of international relations—and this is one of them— the lack of clear-cut consensus, barely tolerable forty years ago, has become intolerably dangerous in the intensified interdependence of a world which has discovered, accumulated, and mobilized the means of exterminating the human race. The ambiguities of the Charter have been made painfully apparent. The Resolutions cited above merely generalize the prohibitions of intervention that have become familiar in the literary output of the Organization of American States, without specifying the elements of that offense. Their inadequacy could not have been better demonstrated than by the invasion of Czechoslovakia in August 1968. Having moved Resolution 2131 (xx), the ussr could hardly

[10] UN Docs. s/6575, August 1, 1965; s/7106, January 31, 1966; s/7168, February 26, 1966.

plead the nonbinding character of such products of the General Assembly. What it could do was to take refuge in a fictitious invitation from the Czech government. As we have seen, such an invitation would, in the doctrine still followed in state practice, remove the invasion from the category of illegal intervention. Once again events proved the necessity of explicitly discarding what has become a farcical pretext for imposing one state's policy upon another. Whenever there is serious internal discord, some faction can be found to invite help from outside, and the faction then figures in the intervening state's brief as the government of the country concerned.

It is perhaps impossible to make any but the simplest and most concrete verbal formulas evasion-proof. But there are degrees of clarity, and it is suggested that decision conducive to peace and welfare in this context would be facilitated by a convention drafted with the technical skill available in the International Law Commission of the United Nations. The convention would be one aiming at the prevention, not the regulation, of unilateral intervention in foreign civil strife. It would prohibit not only fomentation by foreign governments, but also their participation by any action designed to determine the issue and not collectively authorized. It would require that any request for assistance from a government or its opponents must be addressed to collective authority. This authority should be empowered to decide whether or not the situation is serious enough, either as threatening international peace or as involving a flagrant violation of human rights, to warrant collective action that would not constitute an abusive invasion of the state's domestic jurisdiction. Provision should also be made for reference to a tribunal chosen by the disputants, or, failing that, to the International Court of Justice, of disputes arising as to the interpretation or application of the convention. Any action taken by regional organizations in cases

167

of civil strife should be subject to appeal to the universal organization, at present the United Nations.

All this would leave without immediate solution what we have admitted to be the most difficult problem confronting those who seek an effective international order. It is, however, at least a first step toward enforcement to define precisely what is to be enforced. The general concern aroused by the war in Vietnam suggests that it would now be possible to mobilize the majority necessary for a resolution of the General Assembly asking the International Law Commission to prepare a draft. This might resolve the persisting conflicts between competing drafts submitted since 1966 to the Special Committees on Principles of International Law concerning Friendly Relations and Cooperation Among States.[11] The International Law Commission has had vast experience in resolving such conflicts.

The second reason for such a convention now is the educational use that could be made of it. Fifty years of experience in the League of Nations and United Nations leave little doubt that a supranational organization backed by adequate powers of enforcement must await a profound change in political myths. Until it becomes impossible for governments to persuade a majority of their constituents that the continued sovereignty of the state offers a better prospect of peace, security, and welfare than its subordination to collective authority, we cannot expect substantial improvement in the existing restraints upon international violence. The necessary change can only be brought about by a sustained campaign of popular education. Many nongovernmental organizations, national and international, are dedicated to this purpose. Human survival may depend upon their success. Their hand is strengthened by every well designed plan for reinforcing the structure of interna-

[11] See the Special Committee's Report to the General Assembly, 1969, in GAOR, XXIV, supp. no. 19 (A/7619).

tional organization. Even before they have won broad acceptance among governments, such blueprints provide excellent instructional material. Assessment of their strengths and weaknesses and of their place in the general constitution of a world community, enquiry into the reasons why specific governments accept some and reject others—these are only a few of the challenges they present to instructor and student.

INTERNATIONAL PROPAGANDA

Any plan of collective prescription and structure to curb unilateral foreign participation in internal conflict will be confronted with the problem of international propaganda. Radio and television have made this a heavy-caliber, quick-firing weapon of practically unlimited range.

For at least two centuries publicists and interested political leaders have invoked customary norms prohibiting governmental incitement to foreign revolution.[12] It has more recently become common to emphasize the paradox that this limited form of attack should have been held illegal while a positivist age imposed no legal restriction upon all-out war. Since the First World War, hostile, defamatory, warmongering propaganda has been the subject of repeated regional and general conventions and declarations—book law that has had no more visible influence upon actual practice than the alleged customary law.

An attempt was made at the League of Nations Disarmament Conference to impose restraints upon international incitements to violence. That prolonged and frustrated symposium had before it in 1932-1933 a draft treaty that would

[12] For details and bibliography see J. B. Whitton and Arthur Larson, *Propaganda: Towards Disarmament in the War of Words* (Dobbs Ferry, N.Y., 1964) esp. pp. 16-28. In B. S. Murty, *Propaganda and World Public Order* (New Haven, 1968), the history of international propaganda and prescriptions for its control is brought from antiquity up to 1967.

have prohibited propaganda urging one state to declare war upon or to invade another, to attack its territory, its land, its naval or air forces, or to blockade it. Prohibited also would be propaganda in favor of armed bands organized in one state and invading another, or advocating refusal of any request from the target state to prevent aid to such bands. This effort shared the fate of the whole program of the Conference, overtaken as that was by Nazi, Fascist, and Japanese preparations for the Second World War.

The attack on propaganda was nevertheless resumed in 1936, when the Geneva Convention on Broadcasting in the Cause of Peace forbade incitement to acts disturbing the internal order or threatening the security of the signatories, and the broadcasting of appeals for war. The parties also undertook not to disseminate false statements of such a nature as to jeopardize good relations. The obligation to rectify such statements, if made, foreshadowed the right of reply which, as we shall later see, may prove the sole substantial result on the universal plane of years of discussion and negotiation on international propaganda.[13] Regionally, the Latin American states can boast a long series of agreements prohibiting the dissemination of commentary slandering or dishonoring target governments, and the broadcasting of material threatening the sovereignty and integrity of the states parties. Even here, however, the record is not one to encourage hope that this most elusive political instrument can soon be brought under effective control.

Since the Second World War, with its demonstration of the power and the dangers of modern propaganda, the campaign for international control has redoubled. The

[13] The 1936 Convention came into effect in 1938 and was eventually ratified by twenty-two states, of which twelve are still bound. Germany, Italy, and Japan did not sign, and the United States failed to ratify on the ground that it did not control broadcasting. (LNTS, 1938, 186: 309.) Cf. Whitton and Larson, op.cit., p. 70.

Nuremberg Judgment condemned as an international crime propaganda inciting to war, and the Code of Offenses Against the Peace and Security of Mankind, drafted in 1951 by the International Law Commission of the United Nations at the request of the General Assembly, incorporates this finding.[14] In 1947 and 1950, the General Assembly passed Resolutions condemning propaganda "designed or likely to produce or encourage any threat to the peace, breach of the peace, or act of aggression." Resolution Two of the United Nations Conference on Freedom of Information and of the Press, 1948, repeated this condemnation verbatim. In 1952, the General Assembly adopted a draft Convention on the International Right of Correction. This came into force in 1962, after the stipulated sixth ratification, but there have been no further acceptances. As a final item in this selective survey of steps taken under United Nations auspices, we must mention the prohibition of all war propaganda in Article 20 of the draft Covenant on Civil and Political Rights opened for signature at New York on December 19, 1966.

The record is one of many attempts, with very little success, to impose effective restrictions. It does, however, establish the existence of broad formal consensus on the principle that warmongering propaganda is illegal. What is lacking here, as in so many areas of the international order, is a consensus upon means of preventing or arresting violations of the principle. The Western democracies, notably the United States and Great Britain, have usually been markedly unenthusiastic about plans of collective control, fearing, it was said, undesirable limitations upon freedom of speech that might be manipulated by totalitarian regimes to the disadvantage of those trying to maintain fundamental freedoms. The Soviet Union, on the other hand, long played the part of advocate of treaty prohibition of

[14] For text see UNYB, 1952, p. 842.

171

warmongering broadcasts. Yet when President Eisenhower, in his address to the General Assembly on August 13, 1958, proposed that the United Nations should monitor broadcasts in the explosive Near East, it was Mr. Gromyko who poured scorn on the suggestion. At the Eighteen-Nation Disarmament Session at Geneva in May 1962, the United States, in response to urgent proposals from the Russian representative, modified its position sufficiently to join in drafting a Declaration calling upon all states "to adopt, *within the limits of their constitutional systems*," measures to stop "appeals for war and for the settlement of disputes between states by the use of force," and "to promote, *by every means at their disposal*, the widest possible circulation of news, ideas and opinions conducive to the strengthening of peace and friendship among peoples" (my emphasis). The Declaration was adopted unanimously and enthusiastically by the Conference Committee of the Whole on May 25. At the plenary session on May 29, Moscow performed a spectacular *volte-face*. Zorin, on instructions from the Kremlin, withdrew the acceptance given a week earlier in the name of the USSR, and proposed amendments obviously unacceptable to the Western Powers.[15]

What is the explanation of this long series of advances and retreats with nothing greater to show for it than a right of reply more widely recognized than the paucity of formal acceptances might suggest? Does the total answer lie in the ideological and power struggle that is the cold war? Certainly we find here the same declared acceptance of gen-

[15] The text is quoted by Whitton and Larson, *op.cit.*, pp. 234-35, from the *New York Times*, May 26, 1962. I have italicized the passages which doubtless facilitated US participation in this gesture. Washington would always be able to retreat behind its constitutional incapacity to interfere with the state control of broadcasting. For the Soviet withdrawal, see the *New York Times*, May 30, 1962, p. 1. Both the original text and the Soviet amendments that would have made it a propaganda triumph for the USSR are reproduced in Murty, *op.cit.*, pp. 235-37.

eral principles, coupled with the same revulsion from machinery of enforcement, as in the endless negotiations on reduction and control of armaments. And it is far from clear that the United States is any more ready than the Soviet Union for the surrender of this particular arm. Washington has shown itself hardly less determined than Moscow to win acceptance for its system of values, and verbal and pictorial propaganda is a cheaper way of doing that than artillery and bombs.

On the other hand, there is real doubt about the possibility of a collective screening of communications that would stop what is internationally dangerous without forfeiting the values of frank mutual information. The argument is often heard that the best antidote to the poison of vicious propaganda, save perhaps in periods of high tension, is free commentary limited only by the ordinary laws against defamation enforceable in national courts. That this recourse does not satisfy the demand for protection is demonstrated by the recurrence of the problem on the agenda of international conferences.

It is of course open to governments to submit to the Security Council of the United Nations complaints that propaganda from any state is threatening the peace, and it would surely be within the Council's powers under Chapter VII of the Charter to make arrangements for monitoring. Any such measure would be subject to veto, whereupon the General Assembly might be seized of the matter and might recommend steps.[16] Nothing more trenchant than this in the way of sanctions is to be expected short of a general strengthening of the inchoate institutions of world government. The movement to control propaganda thus shares the

[16] Whitton and Larson, op.cit., p. 225, suggest that the General Assembly might by simple majority refuse the representatives of a delinquent member the privilege of speaking from its tribune. Murty, op.cit., p. 270, expresses doubts, which I share, about the Assembly's power so to limit a member's participation in its proceedings.

prospects of the effort to limit national armaments. The two problems are in fact more closely related than the term "moral disarmament" suggests. Any treaty that may eventually be achieved on disarmament might appropriately contain a section on propaganda.

Meanwhile, continued admonitions from United Nations bodies should not be regarded as wasted. They can at least contribute to the growth of a general disapproval of internationally dangerous or offensive broadcasting. Nor need appeals to these bodies be confined to cases where the peace is seriously threatened. An organization whose members are "determined to practice tolerance and live together in peace with one another as good neighbors" must always be open to the complaint that relations are being soured by offensive communications directed or tolerated by one of their governments.[17]

[17] On the whole problem of establishing and maintaining a control that would reduce the risk of violence induced by propaganda without gravely limiting freedom of information, see the admirable work of B. S. Murty, already cited, esp. pp. 286-94.

7.

FROM INTERNATIONAL TO WORLD LAW

IN the last two decades there has been a great outpouring of literature presenting new theories of international law and relations and new approaches to their study. The new directions are apparent in the legal literature of many countries, but the output has been particularly voluminous in the United States, where an elaborate organization of research, operating with immense academic energy, has been dedicated to the enterprise.

Despite some unnecessary obscurity and prolixity of style, the substantive quality of this work has been high. Already an important measure of new understanding of the complex processes of international decision-making has been achieved. Given time, this clarification may expand the role of reason and humanity in the practices of states and lead to increased authority and power in the agencies of world community.

This is not to say that sharpened analysis has generated any marked increase of optimism. The reader will often emerge from his study of contemporary work with the suspicion that today's realism identifies optimism with naïveté. While many of the recent books that record and explain the defeats suffered in international organization also present data demonstrating marked development in both the consciousness and the institutions of a community of mankind, this aspect of the material is not emphasized. Too often, indeed, it is buried in the elaboration of concepts, models, and systems.

It is my purpose in this chapter to sketch from its remote historical beginnings the rise, decline, and reinvigoration of the concept of world community as an operative factor in international relations and in the development of a general normative order. There is no assumption in what follows that an effective universal community, capable of controlling even that leviathan, the nation-state, is just over the horizon, or that man can survive long enough to achieve it. What is attempted is an identification and survey of integrative processes, without calculation of the probability of their completion.

Official and unofficial formulations of general legal orders are but one of the paths of progress. The same can be said of internationally organized efforts to keep the peace. What we have to examine, in addition to these, is a vast complex of more or less disparate activities with more limited objectives. These include governmental and intergovernmental programs aiming at economic and social advancement and the definition of universal human rights, the work of official and unofficial agencies attempting to unify particular parts of national legal systems, and the widespread cooperative activities of such nongovernmental associations as the International Chamber of Commerce. Finally, we must take account of the operations of the great multinational business corporations insofar as these, incidentally or by design, make for worldwide unification of practice and the gradual assimilation of national laws bearing upon commercial and industrial enterprise.

Our time is one of deep pessimism about the possibility of controlling international violence. Just as, twenty years after the First World War, hope and energy had gone out of the League of Nations' effort to ensure peace under law, so now the impulse of 1945 to resume and strengthen that effort seems to have spent itself in the conflict with self-seeking national policies. Whether humanity will continue to prefer the constant risk of extermination to disarmament and the subordination of the state to central authority endowed with power to enforce a common law is a question for prophets. No attempt will be made to answer it here. Happily, men (and women) go on living and working as if they believe that the race has a future. That fact makes it worth while (*a*) to assemble the evidence that, notwithstanding wars hot and cold, the long progression toward integration in a community of mankind has not stopped dead, and (*b*) to identify, where possible, promising lines of advance.

World law is an ancient aspiration. The *jus naturale* and *jus gentium* of the Roman and medieval jurists gave practical expression to the Stoic teaching of a community of man living under a divinely ordained natural law. *Jus gentium* was the name for those norms that were thought to be implanted by nature in the legal orders of all peoples, as distinct from those peculiar to each. It was the Roman and medieval version of what we now call general principles of law, and it was held to be as binding upon princes as upon their subjects. Thus, with usages established by long practice and a growing network of treaties, it served the purposes of our public international law.

This growth of a personally binding world law was interrupted by the sharpening separation of peoples into territorially delimited states asserting an aggressive independence. The governments of these states had been vastly strengthened by the late-medieval reassembly under their authority of the feudal fragmentation that had followed the breakup of the Roman Empire. With the Renaissance came the doctrine of the *populus* as a corporate person replacing the prince as the ultimate repository of sovereignty and making ruling individuals or bodies agents, though glorified agents, of this entity. The subject of the law of nations was coming to be no longer the prince and the ordinary mortal, but the state. *Jus inter gentes* began taking the place of *jus*

177

gentium long before Jeremy Bentham hit upon the term international law. The triumph of positivism in the late eighteenth century made the individual an *object*, not a *subject*, of international law. This law more and more emphasized the separateness of states, making their sovereignty, indeed, its basic principle.

NATIONALISM AND SOVEREIGNTY

Nationalism, internally cohesive, is externally a violently divisive force. Its banner is sovereignty. When, after the war of 1914-1918, the first great essay in international organization was inaugurated, the founding fathers insisted that the League of Nations was no superstate, no world government, but a mere association of sovereign states. Even in 1945, after a second holocaust, the men who drafted the Charter of the United Nations found it necessary to pay lip service to the "sovereign equality of all its members" as a first principle, though the soothing deference of this formula was abandoned in subsequent articles giving special status and authority to the Great Powers.

Since 1945 we have seen nationalism operating, under the slogan of self-determination, with unprecedented vigor and scope. The resulting breakup of empires will not necessarily prove an evil in the long run. Hasty and undiscriminating as it has been, the fragmentation had to come sooner or later as a necessary preliminary to any reintegration acceptable to our era. And, paradoxically enough, the insistent demands of a swarm of new states for industrial development that will lift them from the depths of poverty have, as we shall see, added energy to official moves toward a worldwide economic community. These moves were already gathering strength under the League of Nations. They have taken on new vigor and new dimensions under the United Nations, where immediate assistance in the desired development is accompanied by the promotion of uniform laws to govern the international movement and use of goods, services, and capital upon which so much of human welfare must now depend.

INTERSTATE COOPERATION NOW

Despite the still resounding clamor about sovereignty—that coveted, treasured, and transparent badge of national prestige—surely the most profound difference between the international relations of our day and those of any preceding era is the scope and intensity of interstate cooperation. It is true that the attempt to attain collective security through the international organization of power has suffered disastrous setbacks. Yet it has not been abandoned. It has supplemented and even to some extent replaced the shifting alliances by which states have traditionally sought to avert threats to the national domain. Here is the spearhead of the direct attack upon that "scourge of war" from which the peoples of the United Nations proclaimed their determination "to save succeeding generations" (Charter, Preamble). We ought not to be surprised that decisive success in so revolutionary a break with the past will not be achieved in a generation.

Nor should we forget that the frontal attack was far from being the whole of the Charter's plan for the elimination of war. It prescribed concerted measures to remove the causes of the scourge, among which it identified, in addition to the uncertainties and weaknesses of international law, the poverty, disease, illiteracy, oppression, and discrimination that still prevail in much the greater part of the world's population. In its mission to remove these underlying causes of conflict, the United Nations Organization has become the coordinating center of a multiplicity of intergovernmental enterprises now working to raise the level of material and spiritual welfare among all peoples. This many-sided program is the result of broader understanding and longer-

179

term calculation of the interdependence of human interests. It is building essential foundations for what, given time, may become an effective community of mankind.[1]

DEVELOPMENT AND CODIFICATION OF INTERNATIONAL LAW

In the clarification, development, and codification of public international law, the United Nations' performance already exceeds the entire record of the nineteenth century plus that of the League of Nations. If the number of ratifications is any guide, the foreign offices of the world attach high and immediate value to the Vienna Conventions of 1961 and 1963 on Diplomatic and Consular Relations. In substantive importance, however, these can hardly rank with the four Conventions on the Law of the Sea adopted at Geneva in 1958 after years of preparation by the International Law Commission of the United Nations. These show how far the oceans have come to be regarded as public domain of a world community to which all peoples are to have access but where the claims of states are clearly subordinated to the general interest. Among many manifestations of this outlook, particular attention may be drawn to two. The first is Article 3 in the High Seas Convention, which aims to provide landlocked states with long-needed rights of transit to the coast and the use of ports of exit and entry. This led to the implementing Convention of 1965 on Transit Trade of Landlocked States. The second is the general content of the Convention on Fishing and Conservation of the Living Resources of the High Seas. Here we find, alongside due

[1] The Right Honorable Lester B. Pearson, former prime minister of Canada, and now chairman of IBRD's Commission studying international development policy, has expounded this view in two powerful articles, "Beyond the Nation State" and "Trade, Aid and Peace," *Saturday Review*, February 15 and 22, 1969. It is emphasized in the introduction to the Commission's Report, published in the *New York Times*, October 2, 1969, p. 74.

safeguards for the interests of people specially dependent upon such resources, careful provision for the upkeep and increase of a food supply of vital importance to our exploding world population.

Perhaps equally valuable will be the agreement on the Law of Treaties which has emerged from the final conference on the subject held in 1969. In the years of scholarly labor devoted to the monumental draft and commentary submitted to the preparatory conference of 1968, the International Law Commission again demonstrated its merits not only as an agency for coordinated international research but as a reconciler of contending theses. To have cleared away ambiguities and filled gaps that abounded in the customary rules on treaties must stand as a major contribution to the peaceful intercourse of states.

HUMAN RIGHTS

For all its importance, however, the work done on these great formulations of law designed to govern states has in the main been directed at traditional objectives. A more striking break with tradition has been the persistent official drive for a common law defining and implementing the rights of the individual in every political community.

The fortunes of the Universal Declaration of Human Rights, adopted by the General Assembly at Paris in 1948, have confounded some skeptics, including the author of this book. Widespread adoption of its principles in the recent constitutions of old and new states, and the official use made of the advisory and instructional services offered by the United Nations to states seeking to establish rules and procedures for the protection of the individual against arbitrary authority, go some way toward consoling "idealists" for the halting progress toward binding covenants of human rights. In Europe, moreover, the Declaration inspired the Rome Convention of 1950, which incorporated its essential provisions and established a European Commission and a European Court of Human Rights to implement them. Here we have a working organization supported by sixteen states which receives and deals with petitions from private persons alleging violations of the Convention. Among Western European countries only France and Switzerland stand aloof from this common code which the individual can invoke at need against his own government.

It is more difficult, in the nature of things, to establish such a structure on a worldwide scale than in a limited group of states sharing Western European values and a history of democratic institutions. But the group can at any rate provide a model for other regional associations, and its continued success may speed acceptance of the universal code and organization contemplated in the two Draft Covenants sponsored by the United Nations.

Governments are showing marked reluctance to commit themselves firmly to the far-reaching obligations of the two Draft Covenants approved by the General Assembly in 1966. By December 31, 1968, only thirty-nine states had signed the Covenant on Economic, Social and Cultural Rights and thirty-eight the Covenant on Civil and Political Rights. No Great Power was among the fourteen signatories of the Optional Protocol extending the powers of the proposed Committee on Human Rights. Costa Rica was the one state that had yet ratified either Covenant or the Protocol. The signers of the two Covenants included the USSR and Bielorussian and Ukrainian Republics, but the United States and France were not yet among them.[2]

Over the world at large what is going on is a voluntary and gradual approach to the standards set in the Covenants. Though this approach suffers reversals from time to time in particular states, it may carry us as far on the road to practical application as the ratified Covenants would go,

[2] *Multilateral Treaties, 1968.*

for these are decidedly weak in the matter of adjudication and enforcement. No universal court of human rights is contemplated. The standing Committee provided for in the Covenant on Civil and Political Rights has no power to receive complaints from individuals or even from states unless the party complained of has by declaration or protocol agreed to this procedure. Apart from such voluntary extension of its powers, all that the Committee can do is to receive and comment upon the reports which the states parties must submit on measures taken to implement the Covenant.

In regard to certain specific and critical human needs, the United Nations has awaited neither the voluntary adoption of the Universal Declaration nor the coming into force of the general system blueprinted in the Draft Covenants. Not only has the General Assembly issued numbers of declarations and resolutions in pursuit of its mission to assist "in the realization of human rights and fundamental freedoms for all,"[3] but it has secured the adoption of a series of conventions to remedy particular injustices. Among these I shall mention only those aiming at (a) the abolition of slavery and practices approximating slavery; (b) the protection and settlement of refugees and stateless persons, and the reduction of cases of statelessness; (c) the elimination of all forms of discrimination; and (d) equal rights for women.

Conventions, when ratified, impose legal obligations. It is not generally admitted that declarations or resolutions have the same effect. They are, nevertheless, a by-no-means-negligible mode of pressure, for they throw what is for delinquent states an unwelcome light upon deficiencies and abuses. Moreover, when they urge sanctions, many members of the United Nations are willing to comply. In regard to the Republic of South Africa and Rhodesia, they have been instrumental in bringing into play the formally im-

[3] Charter, Art. 13.1b.

perative procedures of the Security Council. Frequently, backed by large majorities, they emphasize a broad consensus upon the duties of states to those under their jurisdiction. Put in other terms, they express a majority view of what international law requires and, in the absence of a court with general and final jurisdiction, there can be no more authoritative statement of what the law is.

LAW FOR MANKIND

It is now more than ten years since C. W. Jenks argued in his book, *The Common Law of Mankind*, that the traditional definition of international law as a code purporting to govern interstate relations is inadequate. It fails to convey what is now the essential character of international law, namely that is only a part, though a major part, of "the common law of mankind in an early stage of development." I accept this thesis. To me it has long meant that we are witnessing a transition in international legal development from a prolonged stage in which the predominant, not to say exclusive, concern was the regulation of the conduct of states as distinct entities, to one in which equal attention is given to promoting the growth of a body of world law transcending states, and applicable, on a footing of equality, to individuals, corporations, international organizations, and states.

Even at its highest point of development, this corpus of world law can be expected to leave intact much of the content of existing state legal systems. Differences in institutions rooted in cultural differences and not preventing essential economic, social, and political developments should and are likely to remain. In any case, the state, as a local focus of loyalties and agency of territorially limited administration, may well prove indispensable. We may never reach a stage of world government where the central authority will be armed with such powers as are normal in federal systems. But, insofar as universal interests are recognized and brought under collective implementation, the state will necessarily be subordinated to supranational agencies exercising, where persuasion fails, some measure of coercion. This truth must be faced even at the risk of temporarily increasing resistance.

There is, of course, resistance. The transition of which I have spoken is neither smooth nor uninterrupted. It is impeded, even here and there arrested, by egocentric personal or national interests and by sensitive pride in a frequently illusory sovereignty. At best, the forces of progress have to overcome the ponderous inertia of tradition-bound governments and peoples. Some political philosophers, assuming the imposing role of prophecy on the strength of their reading of history, make this inertia respectable and help to consolidate it by the dogmatic assertion that man can never rise above his present faulty political structure. One need not accept this credo of futility.

INTERNATIONAL TRADE AND AID

Whatever the chances of general world government in this twentieth century—and our "realists," with much evidence in their favor, assure us that they are nil—the trend toward an integrated human community under a common law is established. It is manifested by the vastly increased membership of the United Nations and by the participation of 130 governments, acting for such a diversity of peoples, in the codification and human rights programs of the world organization. These enterprises are familiar to students of international relations. What is less familiar is the integrating influence of international trade and investment, aided and supplemented, as this now is, by governmental and intergovernmental programs of foreign aid, technical assistance, and economic development. It is to this that we now turn.

185

Specialists in international law and politics have been accused of ignoring what is undoubtedly one of the most significant phenomena in the spectrum of planned global activity. While it should become clear in what follows that the charge is far from wholly justified, it is true that scientific interest is relatively recent and that much work remains to be done to determine the respective optimum roles of private enterprise, governmental policy, and intergovernmental cooperation in coping with what many have come to consider the most urgent problem of our day. That is, how to create a world economic community mobilizing material and human resources in such a way as to prevent exhaustion of the food supply by an explosively multiplying population and, by ensuring rising standards of life in the impoverished lands of Asia, Africa, and Latin America, to reduce the constant threat to the general peace posed by the ever-widening economic gap between those countries and the richer nations of the North. Something has already been said about the movement in that direction. What is needed is (a) more general understanding of its bearing upon the welfare and security even of the wealthier countries, and (b) the wider and steadier support that such understanding would generate.[4]

THE "NEW LAW MERCHANT"

One challenge to research and education in this immense field is the growth of what has begun to be called the "new law merchant." The old law merchant, from its remote beginnings in the Greek and Roman manuscripts of the Rhodian Sea Law, maintained an evolving common order that imposed duties and conferred rights and liberties upon those internationally engaged in the production and ex-

[4] Increased understanding in the United States is one object of the nongovernmental Overseas Development Council formed under the chairmanship of Eugene R. Black, ex-president of IBRD. (New York Times, March 1, 1969, p. 15.)

change of goods. With the sharpening division of Europe into nation-states insisting upon sovereignty, this common order gave way to national determination of commercial relations and the rights and duties of merchants and shipowners and their agents and employees. The liberties of foreign traders came to depend upon bilateral treaties of friendship and commerce. Only in recent decades has there been a return to the universal outlook of the medieval law merchant.[5] In our century the accelerating search for new sources of raw materials and new markets for industrial products has been responsible for the growth of powerful multinational corporations operating simultaneously in many different countries. These carry on their multifarious activities under concessions that fall into a common pattern and bring with them into underdeveloped countries not only modern methods of industrial production and management but new employer–labor relationships, up-to-date technical training, and contemporary measures of public health and sanitation.

Contracts between governments and foreign companies, like those between business concerns of different nationality, now commonly include arbitration agreements. When disputes arise, these agreements offer the advantages, as compared with adjudication in national courts, of lower costs, greater expedition, less rigid principles of settlement, and greater assurance of impartiality. In international as in national business transactions, recent years have witnessed a notable increase in recourse to this less formal and less formidable way of settling trade and investment disputes.

THE INTERNATIONAL CHAMBER OF COMMERCE

For this, chief credit must go to the International Chamber of Commerce (ICC) which, since its foundation in 1919 as

[5] Cf. C. M. Schmitthoff, "Unification or Harmonization of Law by Means of Standard Contracts and General Conditions," in *International and Comparative Law Quarterly* 17 (July 1968), 563.

"the world federation of businessmen"[6] has made the promotion of arbitration one of its principal activities.[7] Since 1924 the ICC Court of Arbitration at Paris has dealt with more than two thousand disputes, and the annual number goes on growing. In the two-year period 1965-1967, 145 cases were submitted, compared with 120 in 1963-1965. Thirteen percent of the 1965-1967 list involved states or state-controlled bodies. The Court offers ready recourse to individuals and corporations with contractual claims against foreign governments.[8]

Yet it is not in the number of cases submitted or finally disposed of that the ICC takes most satisfaction. What its Council considers a greater achievement is the deterrent effect of its widely adopted standard arbitration clause in contracts between parties of different nationality. The fact that provision is thus made for prompt and equitable settlement acts, the Council believes, to reduce the likelihood that obligations will be evaded. "What matters for international trade," it rightly observes, "is that disputes should not take place."[9]

Proceedings in the tribunals set up under the ICC Court

[6] ICC, *Aims, Programs, Organization,* 1966-1967, p. 3.

[7] It would take much more space than is available here to present even a synoptic account of the work that the ICC has devoted to the unification or harmonization of national laws affecting international business. I have selected its promotion of arbitration because it appeals to me as being thus far the most far-reaching and effective of its many contributions to the growth of world law. In the long run its advocacy and draft of a Code of Fair Treatment for Foreign Investments, its collaboration with IBRD in planning for the eventual international insurance of such investments against political and calamity risks, and its *Standard Contract Terms* (Incoterms) may be counted equally important. Meanwhile, its reports, brochures, and guides constitute an indispensable library not only for its members but also for all students of international trade and its integrative effects.

[8] ICC *Biennial Report,* 1965-1967, p. 39.

[9] ICC *Biennial Report,* 1961-1963, p. 42.

188

of Arbitration are confidential. Reports are not made available unless settlement fails and the case goes on to formal adjudication. Thus we are denied here the body of readily available precedents that might play the part in the growth of a substantive world law of business that interstate arbitration has played in the growth of public international law. But the published ICC *Rules of Conciliation and Arbitration* and the *Guide to* ICC *Arbitration* clearly make for uniform arbitral practice, and it was observed long ago that substantive law may be formed in the interstices of procedure. Privacy doubtless pays off in a greater willingness to make use of the facilities offered by the ICC.[10] In any case, it is not only by maintaining its own institutions that this organization of six thousand companies and fifteen hundred business associations in seventy-five countries is helping to establish arbitration as a principal mode of developing and applying law for a world community. It has actively supported the effort to obtain international consensus on the recognition and enforcement of arbitral awards. The lengthening series of conventions on this subject owes much to ICC initiative and sustained pressure. The series begins with the Convention concluded under League of Nations auspices at Geneva in 1927, and continues, through the United Nations New York Convention of 1958 and the European Convention on International Commercial Arbitration of 1961, to the Convention on the Settlement of Investment Disputes between States and Nationals of Other States drafted and submitted to Governments by the International Bank for Reconstruction and Development (IBRD) in 1965.[11]

[10] But for an eloquent plea for publication of arbitral decisions as a mode of building up the new law of international trade, see René David, "L'Avenir de l'Arbitrage," in Pieter Sanders, ed., *International Arbitration: Liber Amicorum for Martin Domke* (The Hague, 1967 [1968]), pp. 317-18.

[11] On the protection of foreign investments in general, and the role of arbitration in particular, see Ignaz Seidl-Hohenveldern, *In-*

THE IBRD CONVENTION OF 1965

The Convention last named, which is now in force between thirty-two states, including the United States and the United Kingdom, deserves special mention.[12] It establishes a standing intergovernmental organization, the International Center for Settlement of Investment Disputes, at the principal office of the Bank. This is governed by an Administrative Council consisting of one representative of each contracting state who, unless a different person is designated, is that state's governor of the Bank. The president of the Bank is *ex officio* chairman of the Administrative Council. The Center maintains panels of conciliators and arbitrators, and its Administrative Council not only determines the rules of conciliation and arbitral procedure, but is authorized to "exercise such other powers and perform such other functions as it shall determine to be necessary for the implementation of the provisions of this Convention" (Arts. 1-6). This sounds very broad, but it must be noted that the Center's jurisdiction is limited to disputes which the parties "consent in writing to submit" (Art. 25). Once that consent has been given, it may not be withdrawn unilaterally, nor can the parties prevent proceedings by refusing to agree upon an arbitrator or arbitrators. Failing such agreement within ninety days, the Chairman of the Administrative Council appoints the arbitrator or arbitrators necessary to constitute the Arbitral Tribunal for the case (Art. 37 and 38). Like the ICC Court, the Center does not itself arbitrate, it provides the machinery for setting up a tribunal as each case arises. The Tribunal decides any question concerning its competence, but for settlement of the dispute follows "such rules of law as may be agreed to

---

vestitionen in Entwicklungsländern und das Völkerrecht (Cologne, 1963).

[12] The citations and quotations that follow are from the text issued by IBRD on March 18, 1965.

by the parties." If the parties fail to agree on the law to be applied, the Tribunal must apply "the law of the contracting State party to the dispute (including its rules on the conflict of laws)" and any applicable rules of international law (Arts. 41 and 42). Unfortunately this treatment of the problem of the choice of law leaves open an existing trap for the private party when there is no clause in the arbitration agreement specifying the law to be applied. He may find himself exposed by the conflict rules of the contracting state to unforeseen disadvantageous conditions.[13]

Articles 53 and 54 require the contracting states to accept the Tribunal's award as binding and not "subject to any appeal or to any other remedy except those provided for in this Convention." They must recognize awards as if they were final judgments of their own courts. For the contracting states this means giving up any liberty their courts now assert to ignore an arbitral award and deal with the dispute *de novo*. For the party losing in arbitration, it means that he can no longer force the winner to depend for satisfaction upon the judgment of the loser's national court. The Convention would thus remedy an existing weakness in the institution of arbitration.

It may be objected that arbitration is a mode of applying rather than creating law. Arbitration agreements commonly determine what law shall be followed in the settlement of disputes between the parties. It is nonetheless true that the reasoned awards of arbitral tribunals establish a pattern of decision for like cases. Even when reports are not published, the opposing claims become known, and the decision between them reveals at least the basic rule followed. The body of law thus formed by a process of accretion is made

[13] Cf. G. Schwarzenberger, "The Arbitration Pattern and the Protection of Property Abroad," in *Liber Amicorum*, pp. 317-18. See also M. Bothe, "Die Behandlung ausländischer Investitionen in Lateinamerika," in *Zeitschrift für ausländisches öffentliches Recht und Völkerrecht*, 28, nos. 3-4 (November 1968), 731-854.

flexible by a larger injection of equity than is always permissible in formal adjudication.

ECONOMIC DEVELOPMENT AND CULTURAL CHANGE

The "new law merchant" that is thus evolving around the massive operations of private international enterprise assisted by governmental and intergovernmental agencies is now attracting attention from lawyers around the world, while the social and political acculturation accompanying economic modernization has come under intensive study by social and political scientists. Academic institutes have been set up to specialize in these largely new fields. One of the first and most productive of these is the University of Chicago's Research Center in Economic Development and Cultural Change, which publishes the authoritative journal of that name.

The editorial preface to the first number of *Economic Development and Cultural Change*, dated March 1952, emphasized the pioneering nature of the contemplated research. "There is no theory," it observes, "which deals with the problem of economic development and cultural change and which is generally satisfactory to social scientists. The considerable attention which has been devoted to such problems in recent years, therefore, has resulted in disparate insights which illuminate individual trees in a forest whose size, shape, and nature has remained obscure." In this same first number, Professor Bert F. Hoselitz, writing on "Non-Economic Barriers to Economic Development," goes straight to the core of the question we are now considering: ". . . economic development," he points out, "consists not merely in a change of production techniques, but also, in the last resort, in a reorientation of social norms and values" (p. 8). It hardly needs to be said that the "reorientation of social norms" means amendment of the legal

192

system, which incorporates and enforces all norms deemed essential to the preservation of the society's values. The process of amendment reflects and crystallizes the cultural change implied in any reorientation of values.

THE SOVIET UNION AND FOREIGN AID

The spreading interest in the "revolution of modernization" and its complex phenomena that accounts for special programs of research in various Western countries has also penetrated the Communist bloc. The Soviet Union could not stay out of the competition for economic advantage and political favor to be gained by foreign aid, and the Kremlin set its economists and social and political scientists to work on the many-sided problems of development in Asia, Africa, and Latin America. Their studies demonstrate a lively, if somewhat belated, interest in the mutual profits to be won from stimulating and helping to organize and manage production in countries demanding a greater share of the world's wealth. What was not so obviously to be expected is their interest in the less immediately material aspects of development, such as the accompanying changes in mores and law.[14]

Volumes are beginning to be written on the changes in the general culture and, particularly, the legal reforms taking place in the newly independent countries. In any serious attempt to satisfy the universal demand for better living conditions, modern organization for the exploitation of available resources is indispensable, and this cannot be achieved without substantial legislative modernization. Add to this the impact of the campaign for universal human rights, and the conditions for legal renovation are established. Here is an endless challenge to the comparative law-

[14] See the excellent review by Elizabeth K. Valkenier, "Recent Developments in Soviet Research on the Developing Countries," *World Politics*, 20 (July 1968) 644-59.

yer, the theorist on law and society and, no less, to the legal advisers of multinational corporations and of governments. There will be a vast literature on the subject.[15] It must suffice here to say that the changes touch the law of family, property, contract, tort, and crime. Insofar as they approach the standards of freedom, welfare, and dignity set forth in the Universal Declaration and Draft Covenants of Human Rights, they constitute a visible advance towards the world community of law envisaged in those products of the United Nations.

The suspicion of capitalist motives displayed by some recipient governments, combined with balance-of-payment difficulties, swelling military commitments, and internal social crises in the richer nations, has begun to reduce the flow of investment capital and foreign aid to those most in need of modernization. Added to these deterrents are increasing Communist assistance and influence in the underdeveloped world. In the United States, congressional fear that more dollars may merely reinforce a Communist dominance already won has drastically cut foreign aid grants. What is lacking in the richer capitalist and Communist countries alike is a common understanding of the indissoluble connection between economic development, national security, and international peace. Such a general understanding is still far to seek. It presupposes an effective and probably prolonged educational campaign. Insofar as it spreads, it puts an end to the conception of foreign business enterprise and governmental aid as counters in a game for prevailing influence, and generates a will to constructive co-

[15] Some idea of the field to be explored may be gained from Majid Khaduri, "From Religious to National Law," in *Changing Law in Developing Countries*, ed. Ruth N. Anshen (London, 1963); Clive M. Schmitthoff, ed., *The Sources of the Law of International Trade* (New York, 1964); E. I. Nwogugu, *The Legal Problems of Foreign Investment in Developing Countries* (Manchester, England, 1965); Richard D. Robinson, *International Business Policy* (New York, 1964).

operation. This is the proposition that gives major importance to such a work as Robert S. McNamara's *The Essence of Security, Reflections in Office*.[16]

For seven years United States Secretary of Defense, and now President of IBRD, Mr. McNamara drives home his thesis that no accumulation of military hardware and no build-up of military power can by itself win national security or international peace. For him, after seven years of building up the armed strength of the United States, the essence of security is development. His formidable array of statistics leaves no doubt of the connection between poverty and violence. From 1958 to 1966 there were "164 internationally significant outbreaks of violence." In his classification, the rich nations are those with per capita incomes of $750 or more. They are twenty-seven in number and only one of them has had "a major upheaval on its own territory" since 1958. The very poor nations are those with per capita incomes of less than $100. There are thirty-eight of these, and thirty-two of them "have suffered significant conflicts." Between the rich and the very poor come the poor and the middle-income nations. Sixty-nine percent of the poor and forty-eight percent of the middle-income group "suffered serious violence" in the period under review.

Security "implies a minimal measure of order and stability," and this cannot be attained without development, which Mr. McNamara defines as "economic, social and political progress" with a "reasonable standard of living." Unaided, the underdeveloped countries cannot achieve this. Thus economic assistance to those willing and able to use it is for Mr. McNamara an essential condition of order, stability, security, and peace.

THE INTERNATIONAL LABOR ORGANIZATION AND THE
UNIFICATION OF LABOR LAW

Among the many interwoven activities contributing to the growth of world law, few, if any, are more productive than

[16] Harper and Row, 1968.

the work of the ILO. How closely that work ties in with international business enterprise is at once obvious to everyone with any knowledge of the structure and products of the Organization. Established in 1919 and connected with the League of Nations, the ILO had by 1939 won a place for itself that enabled it to survive the League's demise in the Second World War and resume full operations as the first specialized agency associated with the United Nations. Its mixed representation of governments, employers, and workers is an ideal qualification for a massive humanitarian program in social and industrial development. Its conventions and recommendations concerning hours and conditions of labor, employment of women and children, adequate living wages, safety measures in industrial plants, workmen's compensation and insurance, social security, technical education, and freedom of association, go far toward establishing a general legal framework within which the worldwide production of goods and services proceeds.[17]

The first Constitution of the ILO, forming Part XIII of the Treaty of Versailles, begins with a preamble expressing views on the connection between poverty and war that anticipate those voiced fifty years later by Robert S. McNamara. Peace, it declares, "can be established only if it is based upon social justice," whereas "conditions of labour exist involving such injustice, hardship and privation to large numbers of people as to produce unrest so great that

[17] For a full account, see C. W. Jenks, *The International Labor Code* (Geneva, 1952); and the more recent compilation, *Conventions and Recommendations, 1919-1966* (Geneva, 1966). Dr. Jenks's *Human Rights and International Labour Standards* (London, 1960), reflects the breadth of vision that has characterized the direction of the Organization from its beginning. Still worth consulting is Kathleen Gibberd's *The Unregarded Revolution* (London, 1937). The award of the Nobel Peace Prize for 1969 to this Organization was a fitting recognition of great service to humanity at large.

the peace and harmony of the world are imperilled." The object of the Organization, however, as the Preamble goes on to make clear, is not simply to aid in preventing war by attacking one of its causes. Social justice and the general improvement of human life are to be sought for their own sakes. This is emphasized again in the Declaration of Philadelphia in 1946 and the revised Constitution of the same year, where we find the pronouncement that "all human beings, irrespective of race, creed or sex, have the right to pursue both their material well-being and their spiritual development in conditions of freedom and dignity, of economic security, and equal opportunity."

That this stated breadth of purpose was not an empty formula has been proved by the Organization's record. As a particularly good illustration of the scope of its activities outside the normal field of labor legislation, one may cite the Andean Indian Program. There, working as coordinating agency with FAO, WHO, and UNESCO, the ILO has been engaged in an enterprise designed to lift a tribal population of seven million, spread over five states, from endemic destitution to progressively higher levels of living. This called for radical improvements in agriculture, the common means of existence; it called for the elementary institutions of education, of public health and welfare; in a word, for the basic conditions of an approach to modern civilization. The task has now been carried forward to a point where direction can be handed over to the five governments concerned.[18]

THE INTERNATIONAL INSTITUTE FOR THE UNIFICATION OF PRIVATE LAW (THE ROME INSTITUTE OR UNIDROIT)

The general unification of private law is the sole purpose and aim of an organization set up at Rome in 1926 as the

[18] See *Everyman's United Nations*, 7th ed. (New York, 1964), pp. 478-79.

result of an arrangement between the Italian Government and the League of Nations. It now has forty-three state members, twenty-four of them European, eleven Latin American, five Asian, two African, and one, the United States, North American. A large part of its work has been directed to the unification of laws relating to international business transactions. Thus it has prepared drafts of conventions and uniform laws on international sales of goods, international contracts made by correspondence, agency in international trade, arbitration, and international loans; and these initiatives have led to a number of formal international agreements. In recent years, the Rome Institute has broadened its scope by holding periodic conferences of organizations interested in legal unification. Its interests extend far beyond trade and finance into the wide area of human rights; witness its efforts to secure adoption of a uniform law on the enforcement of alimentary and maintenance obligations to persons abroad, its detailed reports upon the treatment of aliens in various countries, and its enquiries into the legal status of women.[19]

THE UNITED NATIONS COMMISSION ON INTERNATIONAL TRADE LAW (UNCITRAL)

This is the latest addition to the various agencies through which the United Nations is promoting harmony among the world's legal systems. Based upon General Assembly Resolution 2102 (xx) of December 20, 1966, it is made up of the representatives of twenty-nine states designated for six-year terms by the General Assembly. The geographical distribution of these countries indicates the intended close connection with the development agencies and programs of the United Nations, especially the Conference on Trade and Development (UNCTAD). Seven are African, five Asian, four

[19] See the Institute publication, *L'Unification du Droit*, with English translation (Rome, 1948).

Eastern European, five Latin American, eight Western European and other.

The Commission held its first meeting, largely an organizing and programming session, at United Nations Headquarters in January and February 1968. The program adopted includes and gives priority to the international sale of goods, commercial arbitration, and international payments. After these will come transportation, insurance, intellectual property, elimination of discrimination, agency, and the legalization of documents. Cooperation with the Rome Institute is planned, and the Commission will press for the widest possible acceptance of such conventions as those concluded at The Hague in 1964—Uniform Laws on the International Sale of Goods and on the Formation of Contracts for the International Sale of Goods. The high priority given arbitration in the program is further proof of the importance attached to that institution.

My survey has, I hope, shown that a marked advance in integration has occurred in the last half century and that despite setbacks it continues. The advance has been carried on by a partly fortuitous combination of private and public enterprise directed to particular tasks without overall definition of purpose or plan of concerted action. If there has been any underlying theory, it is of the functionalist type propounded in the last three decades by David Mitrany and his followers.[20]

In Mitrany's judgment, a universal political authority was neither possible nor necessary. He believed that the proliferation of specialized international agencies, each serving a limited common interest, would eventually make "frontier

[20] See, e.g., David Mitrany, *A Working Peace System*, 4th ed. (London, 1946); Ernest Haas, *Beyond the Nation State* (Stanford, 1964); J. P. Sewell, *Functionalism and World Politics* (Princeton, 1966); Gunnar Myrdal, *Beyond the Social Service State* (New Haven, 1960).

199

lines meaningless by overlaying them with a growth of common activities."

Twenty years of integrative effort in Europe, culminating in 1967 in the fusion of the executive bodies of the Coal and Steel, Atomic Energy, and Economic Communities, hardly encourage such hope. Specialized functions do not flourish automatically and indefinitely without the coordinating control of central political authority.[21] Experience suggests that on the universal plane the step from quantitative integration to qualitative change in the legal distribution of power will demand difficult political decisions, and that it will take a sustained worldwide educational campaign to convince the peoples that effective centralized direction is indispensable.[22]

[21] See F. B. Jensen, *The Common Market; Economic Integration in Europe* (Philadelphia, 1965), esp. ch. 13; Stephen Holt, *The Common Market* (London, 1967).

[22] For a study in depth of the complex processes making for an organized world community, see M. S. McDougal, H. D. Lasswell, and W. M. Reisman, "The World Constitutive Process of Authoritative Decision," in R. A. Falk and C. E. Black, *The Future of the International Legal Order*, 1 (Princeton, 1969), 73-154.

8.

SUMMING UP AND PROSPECT

NO government today openly avows the Hegelian doctrine that the state is the final achievement of man's political genius and that its very nature prohibits its subjection to law. Governments commonly include individuals who would welcome a supranational integration strong enough to maintain peace and ensure the shared economic development that has come to be regarded as a condition of human survival. Even those leaders who privately dismiss projects of effective world organization as illusory rarely take the negative position in public. They find it useful to encourage the hope that through some vague arrangements supported by mutual understanding and common purpose "aggressors" may be brought to book and the rule of law and reign of justice assured. The proclaimed ends are irreproachable, the proposed means woefully inadequate. The ideas dominant in the formation and pursuit of foreign policy are still largely those of the eighteenth and nineteenth centuries. The United States, United Kingdom, and France are hardly less opposed than the Soviet Union to any structure that for the sake of efficiency would subordinate the state to collective authority. All four are governed by men who refuse to accept the evidence that, as an agency of security and welfare, the state in its present panoply of myths and symbols is an anachronism. Rationally, the growing interdependence of all major interests calls for planetary administration. In this the role of the state would be one of territorially and substantively limited government with responsibility to universal authority operating in some areas through regional organization. But to suggest this to the present governments of the Great Powers, or to the majorities that still support them, verges dangerously on treason.

The preceding chapters have sketched official advances towards supranational organization directing services of universal concern. These have been responses to permanent and sharply felt needs that could be met only by collectively ordered action, but for which the necessary organization (usually described as "administrative" and "nonpolitical") did not encroach upon the inner sancta of sovereignty. To some extent these functional enterprises have been coordinated under the United Nations, where their directing bodies figure as specialized agencies "brought into relationship" with the world organization (Charter, Art. 63). It might have been expected that the bulk of funds for the promotion of the shared economic, social, and political development that was coming to be regarded as a condition, not only of general welfare, but of security as well, would be channeled through the United Nations. This would have reduced, if it did not eliminate, the competition between the Great Powers to purchase, by foreign aid, economic, political, and strategic advantages in the swarm of new nations born in a precipitate decolonization. By the same token, it would have freed the desperately needed assistance from the jealousy of "neo-imperialism" that has begun seriously to hamper the desired development. As it is, foreign aid has become in large and wasteful measure a weapon of the cold war.

Happily, shared development in a worldwide community does not have to depend wholly upon governments and their international agencies. Multinational business corporations, assisted by such nongovernmental associations

202

as the International Chamber of Commerce, are taking a part that looks beyond immediate gain and accepts social service as an essential condition of long-term profits. We have seen how their operations are making for the more efficient exploitation of natural resources through the modernization of industrial methods, employer–labor relations, technical education, and public health measures. Accompanying this is a modernization and assimilation of national legal systems designed to remove cultural obstacles to the satisfaction of insistent demands for higher standards of living.

In the field of human rights the twenty-year drive to convert the Universal Declaration of 1948 into binding conventions has ended in the weak compromises of the two Draft Covenants adopted by the General Assembly of the United Nations in 1966. A less coercive order for this sensitive area of sovereignty could hardly have been contrived. Yet so wary are governments of external interference in their relations with their nationals that in the three years in which these Covenants have been awaiting ratification (1969) only six states have deposited their instruments of acceptance. The record has its uses as a gauge of official attitudes towards supranational authority. It does not mean that the long campaign for a system that would make of every human being a legally protected citizen of a world community transcending states has come to a halt. The "action program" is still with us, and states continue to adapt their laws to the standards of the Declaration. It does mean that progress towards these standards on the universal plane remains a matter of national discretion, and that ratification of a pair of Covenants that make no provision for adjudication or for effective action against delinquent states will not materially alter this situation. Regionally, the vigor of the European system established by the Rome Convention of 1950 and subsequent Protocols may stimulate more decisive

203

measures. The Organization of American States has clearly been stirred to emulation. The comparative homogeneity of neighboring cultures suggests that in this vital part of the struggle for human advancement the regional approach may be the path of achievement.

Meanwhile a number of interdependent developments has stimulated renewed effort to devise means of controlling international violence. A wave of horror over the murder, destruction, and brutalizing effects of the wars in Vietnam, Nigeria, and the Middle East has brought new vigor and a fresh cause to the revolt against authority now sweeping around the world. The waste of resources in the armaments race, and the resulting inability to cope effectively with multiplying internal problems, have moved the United States and the Soviet Union to more serious efforts to stop a senseless escalation. In 1962 both Powers submitted to the Eighteen-Nation Disarmament Committee at Geneva elaborate proposals to that end; but stubborn differences in regard to the composition and authority of controlling bodies and their methods of supervision prevented the fusion of these blueprints into one common plan. Since that time some minor advances have been made. Tests of nuclear weapons in the atmosphere were prohibited by the Partial Test Ban Treaty of 1963, and the United States and Soviet Union ratified in 1969 a treaty to prevent the spread of these weapons to states not already possessing them. This latter agreement was signed by nonnuclear states on the understanding that nonproliferation would pave the way for the general nuclear disarmament which the signatories pledged themselves to promote in the Preamble and in Article VI. The Soviet-American negotiations that began at Helsinki in November 1969, were in part a move to honor this pledge.

Should these negotiations lead to an organization capable of ensuring the reduction and eventual elimination of nuclear weapons, this would go a long way toward the prevention of war. Only a major breakthrough in the long conflict between sovereignty and security could ensure effective agencies of control, and it would then be a relatively short step to the reduction of all national armaments to a police level and the establishment of supranational institutions strong enough to control resort to force among states. The widest of all the gaps in the world rule of law would be filled.

INDEX

207

209

Republic, 120-121, 123, 126, 151; and economic development, 129-131; and Guatemala, 145-146; and Haiti, 120, 125-126; and hemisphere defense, 118, 120, 122, 124; and human rights, 125-126, 129, 204; and ICJ, 119, 129; and intervention, 123, 127, 155; and pacific settlement, 118-120; and recognition of new governments, 129; and sanctions, 120, 121-123; and the UN, 129, 145-151

instruments and organizations: Alliance for Progress, 130-131; Bogota Charter, 118-120; and Protocol of Amendment, 124; Bogota Pact, 118-120; Commission of Jurists and the development of international law, 118, 126-129; Convention on Civil Aviation, 127-128; Council, 120-122; Declaration of Caracas (1954), 149; Economic and Social Council, 130; Inter-American Commission on Human Rights, 125-126; Inter-American Common Market, 131; Inter-American Council of Jurists, 128; Inter-American Juridical Committee, 128; Inter-American Peace Committee, 124-125; Inter-American Treaty of Reciprocal Assistance (Rio Treaty, 1947), 118, 120, 148-149; Montevideo Convention on Rights and Duties of States, 66, 123n, 128; Organ of Consultation, 120-122; Pan-American Union, 117

Padelford, Norman J., 107n
peace treaties (1919-1920), and the League of Nations Covenant, 95
peaceful coexistence, 57-58
Pearson, Lester B., 180n
Permanent Court of Arbitration, 35, 94
Permanent Court of International Justice (PCIJ), 23, 95-96; authority of judgments and advisory opinions, 45; jurisdiction, 23, 50; Statute, 45
judgments and opinions: *Danzig Railway Officials, Eastern Greenland, The Lotus, Tunis and Morocco Nationality Decrees*, 45-46, 76
Philippines, in Vietnam, 163
piracy, 77
populus, as sovereign, 177
positivism, 34; recent criticism of, 48-49
poverty and violence, 194-195, 196-197
propaganda, 169-174; Convention on the International Right of Correction, 171; draft Code of Offenses against the Peace and Security of Mankind, 171; draft Covenant on Civil and Political Rights, 171; draft Declaration at Eighteen-Nation Disarmament Session (1962), 172; Geneva Convention on Broadcasting in the Cause of Peace, 170; Latin-American agreements on, 170; proposals to monitor broadcasts, 172, 173; right of reply, 170, 171, 173; UN resolutions on, 171
Pufendorf, Samuel, 34